BEST-EVER RECIPES
JAPANESE & SUSHI

BEST-EVER RECIPES
JAPANESE & SUSHI

THE AUTHENTIC TASTE OF JAPAN: 100 TIMELESS CLASSIC AND REGIONAL RECIPES SHOWN IN OVER 300 STUNNING PHOTOGRAPHS

Emi Kazuko

Yasuko Fukuoka

HERMES
HOUSE

This edition is published by Hermes House, an imprint of Anness Publishing Ltd, Blaby Road, Wigston, Leicestershire LE18 4SE
Email: info@anness.com
Web: www.hermeshouse.com;
www.annesspublishing.com

www.hermeshouse.com; www.annesspublishing.com

If you like the images in this book and would like to investigate using them for publishing, promotions or advertising, please visit our website www.practicalpictures.com for more information.

Publisher: Joanna Lorenz
Senior Managing Editor: Conor Kilgallon
Text: Emi Kazuko
Recipes: Yasuko Fukuoka
Photography: Craig Robertson (recipes) and Janine Hosegood (reference section)
Food for photography: Julie Beresford, assisted by Atsuko Console (recipe section); and Annabel Ford (reference section)
Stylist: Helen Trent
Production Controller: Steve Lang
Design: The Bridgewater Book Company Ltd

The publisher would like to thank the following picture libraries for the use of their pictures in the book. Every effort has been made to acknowledge the pictures properly, however we apologize if there are any unintentional omissions, which will be corrected in future editions.

Picture credits
All images copyright Anness Publishing Ltd except The Art Archive p158; Cephas Picture Library p159, p161m, p163.

ETHICAL TRADING POLICY
At Anness Publishing we believe that business should be conducted in an ethical and ecologically sustainable way, with respect for the environment and a proper regard to the replacement of the natural resources we employ.

As a publisher, we use a lot of wood pulp in high-quality paper for printing, and that wood commonly comes from spruce trees. We are therefore currently growing more than 750,000 trees in three Scottish forest plantations: Berrymoss (130 hectares/320 acres), West Touxhill (125 hectares/305 acres) and Deveron Forest (75 hectares/185 acres). The forests we manage contain more than 3.5 times the number of trees employed each year in making paper for the books we manufacture.

Because of this ongoing ecological investment programme, you, as our customer, can have the pleasure and reassurance of knowing that a tree is being cultivated on your behalf to naturally replace the materials used to make the book you are holding. Our forestry programme is run in accordance with the UK Woodland Assurance Scheme (UKWAS) and will be certified by the internationally recognized Forest Stewardship Council (FSC). The FSC is a non-government organization dedicated to promoting responsible management of the world's forests. Certification ensures forests are managed in an environmentally sustainable and socially responsible way. For further information about this scheme, go to www.annesspublishing.com/trees

© Anness Publishing Ltd 2011

A CIP catalogue record for this book is available from the British Library.

Many of the recipes in this book previously appeared in *Japanese Cooking* by Emi Kazuko and Yasuko Fukuoka

NOTES
For all recipes, quantities are given in both metric and imperial measures and, where appropriate, in standard cups and spoons. Follow one set of measures, but not a mixture, because they are not interchangeable.
Standard spoon and cup measures are level. 1 tsp = 5ml, 1 tbsp = 15ml, 1 cup = 250ml/8fl oz.
Australian standard tablespoons are 20ml. Australian readers should use 3 tsp in place of 1 tbsp for measuring small quantities.
American pints are 16fl oz/2 cups. American readers should use 20fl oz/2.5 cups in place of 1 pint when measuring liquids.
Electric oven temperatures in this book are for conventional ovens. When using a fan oven, the temperature will probably need to be reduced by about 10–20°C/20–40°F. Since ovens vary, you should check with your manufacturer's instruction book for guidance.
The nutritional analysis given for each recipe is calculated per portion (i.e. serving or item), unless otherwise stated. If the recipe gives a range, such as Serves 4–6, then the nutritional analysis will be for the smaller portion size, i.e. 6 servings. Measurements for sodium do not include salt added to taste.
Medium (US large) eggs are used unless otherwise stated.
Front cover shows Deep-Fried and Marinated Small Fish – for recipe, see page 121.

Contents

Introduction

To many people, Japan is an exciting and exotic country, mixing tradition and modernity to striking effect. Its cuisine is no exception, and in many ways reflects Japanese culture. The minimalism in aesthetics, such as poetry and music, is also evident in the presentation of food.

FRESHNESS AND SIMPLICITY

One of the defining features of the Japanese cuisine is the relationship between food and nature. Whenever possible, food is eaten in as natural a state as possible, as this is considered the best, if not the only way to experience the true taste of food. This is at the heart of the Japanese philosophy of eating, so the fish and shellfish caught in the seas of Japan are often eaten raw, or lightly cured with vinegar or salt.

Fresh, seasonal agricultural products are only lightly cooked to preserve their bite and flavour, or they may be slightly salted.

How and what people cook is also highly influenced by the season and by local produce. Many regional dishes exist that have been inspired by food that has been produced locally.

Japanese cooking retains the fresh quality of vegetables and rarely mixes different food types. Sauces are served in separate dishes as dips. This contrasts with other cuisines that use long, slow cooking techniques, often with the addition of sauces and spices.

ARTISTIC PRESENTATION

The Japanese aesthetic regarding food and drink may be described in artistic terms, and Japanese cooking can be compared to the *ukiyo-e* woodblock prints. The beauty of the *ukiyo-e* style lies in its economy of line and simplicity, and it is this same elegant minimalism that is found in all good Japanese cooking.

The unique approach of Japanese chefs helped to inspire French chefs in the 1970s to develop nouvelle cuisine, in which food was artistically arranged on the plate. However, nouvelle cuisine became notorious for its overemphasis on presentation rather than the size of the serving, forgetting the essential fact that Japanese meals consist of several, not just a few, small dishes.

ABOVE: *How a dish of* sashimi *is arranged is as important as the freshness of the fish.*

ABOVE: *Fresh seasonal vegetables are chosen and cooked with care.*

ABOVE: *A cooking technique called* tataki *is used to cook rare steak.*

CULTURAL DIFFERENCES

It is interesting to observe how Japan's food culture has developed differently to those of its neighbours, particularly China's. For instance, while many of the same herbs, spices, flavourings and sauces are used in both Chinese and Japanese cooking, the dishes produced by Japanese styles of cooking are quite different to the Chinese styles of cooking. Buddhism is also present in both countries, but in Japan it has led to the development of the tea ceremony and *cha-kaiseki*, the formal meal that is served with it, and these two elements – the tea ceremony and the formal meal – are unique to the Japanese cuisine.

USING THIS BOOK

As Japanese dishes are often served raw or only lightly cooked, careful selection and preparation of fresh ingredients is one of the most important aspects of Japanese cooking, and is also where a real part of the pleasure resides. No special knowledge is needed to make the recipes, and, apart from a few absolute essentials, such as a pair of chopsticks, most cooks will easily be able to prepare and cook Japanese recipes with minimal fuss using the kitchen equipment that they already possess.

The recipes in this book offer the best of local and national Japanese cuisine, from simple sushi appetizers and noodle dishes to delicious and filling hotpots and the most popular desserts. As they say in Japan, just heed what nature is offering and enjoy.

Sushi and rice

In Japanese cuisine, sushi means dishes

that use su-meshi, a slightly sticky rice

that is seasoned with vinegar before

moulding. Many kinds of fish or vegetables

are used in sushi dishes. Because rice is so

popular in Japan, it is also shaped into

rice balls, added to soups, or served with

fish or meat dishes. Delicious recipes in

this chapter include su-meshi in Tofu Bags

and Red Rice Wrapped in Oak Leaves.

Hand-rolled sushi

This is a fun way to enjoy sushi. Called Temaki-zushi, *meaning hand-rolled, each guest rolls together individual fillings of fish and shellfish, vegetables and* su-meshi.

SERVES 4–6

2 quantities *su-meshi* (see page 171), made with 40ml/8 tsp caster (superfine) sugar

225g/8oz extremely fresh tuna steak

130g/4$\frac{1}{2}$oz smoked salmon

17cm/6$\frac{1}{2}$in Japanese cucumber or salad cucumber

8 raw king prawns (jumbo shrimp) or large tiger prawns, peeled

1 avocado

7.5ml/1$\frac{1}{2}$ tsp lemon juice

20 chives, trimmed and chopped into 6cm/2$\frac{1}{2}$in lengths

1 packet mustard and cress, roots cut off

6–8 shiso leaves, cut in half lengthways

TO SERVE

12 nori sheets, cut into four

mayonnaise

shoyu

45ml/3 tbsp wasabi paste from a tube, or the same amount of wasabi powder mixed with 15ml/1 tbsp water

gari

1 Put the *su-meshi* into a large serving bowl, then cover it with a damp dish towel.

2 Slice the tuna, with the grain, into 5mm/$\frac{1}{4}$in slices then into 1 x 6cm/$\frac{1}{2}$ x 2$\frac{1}{2}$in strips. Cut the salmon and cucumber into strips the same size as the tuna.

3 Insert bamboo skewers into the prawns, then boil in lightly salted water for 2 minutes. Drain and leave to cool. Remove the skewers and cut in half lengthways. Remove the vein.

4 Halve the avocado and remove the stone (pit). Cut into long strips. Sprinkle with the lemon juice.

5 Arrange the fish, shellfish, avocado and vegetables on a plate. Place the nori sheets on a few plates and put the mayonnaise into a bowl. Put the shoyu in individual bowls, and the wasabi paste in a dish. Heap the gari in a small bowl. Half-fill a glass with water and place four to six rice paddles inside.

6 Roll the sushi as follows: take a sheet of nori on the palm, scoop out 45ml/3 tbsp rice and spread it on the nori sheet. Spread some wasabi in the middle of the rice, then place a few strips of different fillings on top. Roll it up as a cone and dip into the shoyu. Have gari between rolls to refresh the mouth.

Nutritional information per portion: Energy 191kcal/797kJ; Protein 8.2g; Carbohydrate 21.3g, of which sugars 7.7g; Fat 8.2g, of which saturates 1.4g; Cholesterol 19mg; Calcium 26mg; Fibre 0.9g; Sodium 442mg.

Hand-moulded sushi

Originally developed in Tokyo as street finger food, Nigiri-zushi *is prepared with a selection of the freshest of fish and eaten within a few minutes of making.*

SERVES 4

4 raw king prawns (jumbo shrimp), head
    and shell removed, tails intact
4 scallops, white muscle only
425g/15oz assorted fresh seafood,
    skinned, cleaned and filleted
2 quantities *su-meshi*
15ml/1 tbsp rice vinegar, for moulding
45ml/3 tbsp wasabi paste from a tube, or
    the same amount of wasabi powder
    mixed with 15ml/1 tbsp water
salt
shoyu and gari, to serve

1 Insert a bamboo skewer into each prawn lengthways. Boil in salted water for 2 minutes. Drain and cool, then pull out the skewers. Cut open from the belly side but do not slice in two. Remove the vein and discard. Open out flat and place on a tray.

2 Slice the scallops horizontally in half, but not quite through. Place on the tray, cut-side down. Cut all the fish fillets into small pieces. Cover the tray, then chill.

3 Place the *su-meshi* in a bowl. Fill a bowl with water and the vinegar.

Wet your hand with the vinegared water. Scoop 25ml/1½ tbsp into your palm. Make a rectangular block with the *su-meshi*.

4 Put the *su-meshi* block on a damp board. Rub a little wasabi paste in the middle of a piece of topping. Put a *su-meshi* block on top of the fish slice and press it. Form your palm into a cup and shape the *nigiri-zushi* to a smooth mound. Place it on a tray. Repeat until all of the rice and toppings are used. Serve with shoyu. Eat a little gari between each sushi to refresh your mouth.

Nutritional information per portion: Energy 392kcal/1636kJ; Protein 29.3g; Carbohydrate 40.5g, of which sugars 0.2g; Fat 12.2g, of which saturates 2.1g; Cholesterol 77mg; Calcium 45mg; Fibre 0.1g; Sodium 86mg.

Jewel-box sushi

Chirashi is the most common form of sushi eaten at home in Japan. A lacquered container is filled with su-meshi, and various colourful toppings are arranged on top.

SERVES 4

2 eggs, beaten
vegetable oil, for frying
50g/2oz mangetouts (snow peas),
    trimmed
1 nori sheet
15ml/1 tbsp shoyu
15ml/1 tbsp wasabi paste from a tube, or
    the same amount of wasabi powder
    mixed with 10ml/2 tsp water
1¼ quantities *su-meshi* made with 40ml/
    8 tsp sugar
salt
30–60ml/2–4 tbsp ikura, to garnish

FOR THE FISH AND SHELLFISH TOPPINGS
115g/4oz very fresh tuna steak, skin
    removed
90g/3½oz fresh squid, body only,
    cleaned and boned
4 raw king prawns (jumbo shrimp), heads
    and shells removed, tails intact

FOR THE SHIITAKE
8 dried shiitake mushrooms, soaked in
    350ml/12fl oz/1½ cups water for
    4 hours, stalks removed
15ml/1 tbsp caster (superfine) sugar
60ml/4 tbsp mirin
45ml/3 tbsp shoyu

1 Slice the fresh tuna steak across the grain, so that it is cut into 7.5 x 4cm/ 3 x 1½in pieces, 5mm/¼in thick. Slice the fresh squid crossways into 5mm/¼in strips. Place both the tuna and squid on a tray, cover them and leave to chill.

2 Pour the shiitake soaking water into a pan, add the shiitake and bring to the boil. Skim the surface and reduce the heat. Cook for 20 minutes, then add the sugar. Reduce the heat and add the mirin and shoyu. Simmer until almost all the liquid has evaporated. Drain and slice thinly.

3 Boil the prawns in salted water for 2 minutes. Drain and cool. Cut open from the belly side but do not slice in two. Remove the black vein. Open out and add to the tray.

4 Beat the eggs and add a pinch of salt. Heat a little oil in a frying pan until it smokes. Wipe away the excess oil, tilt the pan and add enough egg to cover the bottom. Cook until the edge is dry and curling. Turn the omelette over. After 30 seconds, transfer to a board. Use the remaining egg mixture to make several more omelettes. Pile them up, roll then together into a tube and slice very thinly to make strands.

5 Par-boil the mangetouts for 2 minutes, then drain. Cut into 3mm/⅛in diagonal strips. Snip the nori into fine shreds. Mix with the shoyu and wasabi.

6 Divide half the *su-meshi* among four large rice bowls. Spread a quarter of the nori mixture over each bowl. Cover with the rest of the *su-meshi*. Flatten the surface with a wet spatula.

7 Sprinkle over egg strands to cover the surface. Arrange the tuna slices in a fan shape with a fan of shiitake on top. Place a prawn next to the tuna, and arrange the squid strips in a heap on the other side. Arrange the mangetouts and ikura on top.

Nutritional information per portion: Energy 384kcal/1609kJ; Protein 23.1g; Carbohydrate 57.3g, of which sugars 7g; Fat 5g, of which saturates 1.3g; Cholesterol 203mg; Calcium 61mg; Fibre 0.4g; Sodium 1191mg.

Marinated mackerel sushi

Fresh mackerel fillets are marinated, then packed into a mould with sushi rice to make Saba-zushi. Start preparations 8 hours in advance to allow the fish to absorb the salt.

MAKES ABOUT 12

500g/1¼lb mackerel, filleted
salt
rice vinegar
2cm/¾in fresh root ginger, peeled and
    finely grated, to garnish
shoyu, to serve

**FOR THE *SU-MESHI*
(VINEGARED RICE)**
200g/7oz/1 cup Japanese short grain rice
40ml/8 tsp rice vinegar
20ml/4 tsp caster (superfine) sugar
5ml/1 tsp salt

1 Place the fillets skin side down in a flat dish, cover with a thick layer of salt, and leave to stand for at least 3–5 hours.

2 To make the *su-meshi*, put the rice in a large bowl and wash in several changes of water, until it runs clear. Tip into a sieve and leave to drain for 1 hour. Put the rice into a deep pan and add 250ml/8fl oz/1 cup water. Cover and bring to the boil. Reduce the heat and simmer for 12 minutes without lifting the lid. Remove from the heat and leave for 10 minutes.

3 Transfer the rice to a wet Japanese rice tub or large bowl. In a bowl, mix the vinegar, sugar and salt until dissolved. Add to the rice, fluffing it with a wet spatula. Cover with wet dish towels and cool.

4 Wipe the salt from the mackerel. Remove all remaining bones with tweezers. Lift the skin at the tail end of each fillet and peel towards the head end. Place the fillets in a dish, and pour in enough rice vinegar to cover the fish. Leave for 20 minutes, then drain and wipe dry.

5 Line a 25 x 7.5 x 4cm/10 x 3 x 1½in container with clear film (plastic wrap). Lay the fillets in the container, skinned side down, and fill the gaps with the remaining mackerel. Put the *su-meshi* into the container and press down. Cover with the clear film and place a weight on top. Leave overnight.

6 Slice the sushi into 2cm/¾in pieces. Garnish with ginger and serve with shoyu.

Nutritional information per portion: Energy 158kcal/659kJ; Protein 9g; Carbohydrate 15g, of which sugars 1.7g; Fat 6.8g, of which saturates 1.4g; Cholesterol 23mg; Calcium 9mg; Fibre 0g; Sodium 190mg.

Su-meshi in **tofu bags**

Abura-age *(fried thin tofu)* is different to other tofu products. It can be opened up like a bag, and in this recipe it is served with soy sauce-based seasonings and filled with su-meshi.

SERVES 4

8 fresh abura-age or 275g/10oz can
   ready-to-use abura-age (contains
   16 halves)
900ml/1^1/$_2$ pints/3^3/$_4$ cups second dashi
   stock, or the same amount of water
   and 10ml/2 tsp dashi-no-moto
90ml/6 tbsp caster (superfine) sugar

30ml/2 tbsp sake
70ml/4^1/$_2$ tbsp shoyu
generous 1 quantity *su-meshi*, made with
   40ml/8 tsp sugar
30ml/2 tbsp toasted white sesame seeds
gari, to garnish

1 Par-boil the fresh abura-age in rapidly boiling water for about 1 minute. Drain under running water and leave to cool. Squeeze the excess water out gently. Cut each sheet in half and carefully pull open the cut end to make bags. If you are using canned abura-age, drain the liquid.

2 Lay the abura-age bags in a large pan. Pour in the dashi stock to cover and bring to the boil. Reduce the heat and cover, then simmer for 20 minutes. Add the sugar in three batches during this time, shaking the pan to dissolve it. Simmer for a further 15 minutes.

3 Add the sake. Shake the pan again, and add the shoyu in three batches. Simmer until almost all the liquid has evaporated. Transfer the abura-age to a wide sieve and leave to drain.

4 Mix the *su-meshi* and sesame seeds in a wet mixing bowl. Wet your hands and take a little *su-meshi*. Shape it into a rectangular block. Open one abura-age bag and insert the block. Press the edges together to close the bag. Once all the bags have been filled, place them on a large serving plate with the bottom of the bag on top. Garnish with gari.

Nutritional information per portion: Energy 495kcal/2073kJ; Protein 20.5g; Carbohydrate 65.2g, of which sugars 34.5g; Fat 16.7g, of which saturates 0.6g; Cholesterol 0mg; Calcium 1093mg; Fibre 0.6g; Sodium 13mg.

Red rice wrapped in oak leaves

This sticky rice dish, Sekihan, is cooked for special occasions and takes 8 hours to prepare. Edible kashiwa (oak) leaves are used when red rice is prepared for a boy-child's festival.

SERVES 4

65g/2½oz/⅓ cup dried azuki beans
5ml/1 tsp salt
300g/11oz/1½ cups mochigome
50g/2oz/¼ cup Japanese short grain rice
12 kashiwa leaves (optional)

FOR THE *GOMA-SHIO*
45ml/3 tbsp sesame seeds (black sesame,
  if available)
5ml/1 tsp ground sea salt

1 Put the azuki beans in a pan and pour in 400ml/14fl oz/1⅔ cups plus 20ml/4 tsp water. Bring to the boil, reduce the heat and simmer, covered, for 20–30 minutes until the beans look swollen but are still firm. Drain and reserve the liquid, then add the salt. Return the beans to the pan.

2 Wash the two rices together. Drain in a sieve and leave for 30 minutes. Bring another 400ml/ 14fl oz/1⅔ cups plus 20ml/4 tsp water to the boil. Add to the beans and boil, then simmer for 30 minutes. Drain and add the liquid to the bowl with the reserved liquid. Cover the beans and cool. Add the rice to the bean liquid and soak for 4–5 hours. Drain the rice and reserve the liquid. Mix the beans into the rice.

3 Bring a steamer of water to the boil. Turn off the heat. Place a tall glass upside down in the centre. Pour the rice and beans into the steamer and pull the glass out. Steam on high for 10 minutes. Sprinkle the rice mixture with the reserved liquid from the bowl. Cover and repeat the process twice more at 10 minute intervals, then steam for 15 minutes more. Leave to stand for 10 minutes.

4 Make the *goma-shio*. Roast the sesame seeds and salt in a dry frying pan until the seeds start to pop. Cool, then put in a dish.

5 Wipe each kashiwa leaf with a wet dish towel. Scoop 120ml/4fl oz/½ cup of the rice mixture into a wet tea cup and press with wet fingers. Turn the cup upside down and shape the rice into a flat ball. Insert into a leaf folded in two. Repeat until all the leaves are used. Alternatively, transfer the red rice to a large bowl wiped with a wet towel. Serve with a sprinkle of *goma-shio*.

Nutritional information per portion: Energy 432kcal/1807kJ; Protein 12.4g; Carbohydrate 78.7g, of which sugars 0.5g; Fat 7.2g, of which saturates 1g; Cholesterol 0mg; Calcium 105mg; Fibre 2.2g; Sodium 496mg.

Lunch-box rice with three toppings

San-shoku Bento *is a typical* bento *(lunch box) menu for Japanese children. Colourful toppings and a variety of tastes hold their attention so they don't get bored.*

MAKES 4 LUNCH BOXES

275g/10oz/1¹/₂ cups Japanese short
   grain rice cooked using 375ml/13fl oz/
   1²/₃ cups water, cooled
45ml/3 tbsp sesame seeds, toasted
salt
3 mangetouts (snow peas), to garnish

FOR THE *IRI-TAMAGO*
30ml/2 tbsp caster (superfine) sugar
5ml/1 tsp salt
3 large (US extra large) eggs, beaten

FOR THE *DENBU*
115g/4oz cod fillet, skinned and boned
20ml/4 tsp caster (superfine) sugar
5ml/1 tsp salt
5ml/1 tsp sake
2 drops of red vegetable colouring, diluted

FOR THE *TORI-SOBORO*
200g/7oz minced (ground) raw chicken
45ml/3 tbsp sake
15ml/1 tbsp caster (superfine) sugar
15ml/1 tbsp shoyu
15ml/1 tbsp water

1 To make the *iri-tamago*, add the sugar and salt to the eggs in a pan. Cook over a medium heat, stirring. When almost set, remove from the heat and stir until the egg is fine and slightly dry.

2 To make the *denbu*, cook the cod for 2 minutes in a pan of boiling water. Drain and dry well. Skin and remove all the bones. Put the cod and sugar into a clean pan, add the salt and sake, and cook over a low heat for 1 minute, stirring with a fork to flake the cod. Reduce the heat and sprinkle on the colouring. Stir for 15–20 minutes until the cod becomes fluffy and fibrous.

3 For the *tori-soboro*, put the chicken, sake, sugar, shoyu and water into a pan. Cook over a medium heat for 3 minutes, before reducing the heat and stirring until the liquid has almost evaporated.

4 Blanch the mangetouts for 3 minutes, then drain and slice. Mix the rice with the sesame seeds. Divide the rice among four lunch boxes. Flatten the surface with the back of a spoon.

5 Spoon a quarter of the cooked egg mixture into each box to cover a third of the rice. Cover the next third with a quarter of the *denbu* and the last section with a quarter of the chicken. Garnish each topping with the mangetout sticks.

Nutritional information per portion: Energy 515kcal/2160kJ; Protein 29.3g; Carbohydrate 72.3g, of which sugars 17.4g; Fat 11.8g, of which saturates 2.3g; Cholesterol 191mg; Calcium 125mg; Fibre 0.9g; Sodium 862mg.

Rice balls with four fillings

*Onigiri, **the Japanese name for this dish, means hand-moulded rice. Japanese rice is ideal for making rice balls, which are filled here with salmon, mackerel, umeboshi and olives.***

SERVES 4

50g/2oz salmon fillet, skinned
3 umeboshi, 50g/2oz in total weight
45ml/3 tbsp sesame seeds
2.5ml/½ tsp mirin
50g/2oz smoked mackerel fillet
2 nori sheets, each cut into 8 strips

6 pitted black olives, wiped and finely chopped
fine salt
Japanese pickles, to serve

FOR THE RICE
450g/1lb/2¼ cups Japanese short grain rice
550ml/18fl oz/2½ cups water

1 Wash the rice, drain and put into a pan. Add the water and leave for 30 minutes. Cover and bring to the boil. Reduce the heat and simmer for 12 minutes. When you hear a crackling noise remove from the heat and leave, covered, for 15 minutes. Stir with a wooden spatula and cool for 30 minutes. Salt the salmon and leave for 30 minutes. Stone (pit) the umeboshi then mash them slightly. Mix with 15ml/1 tbsp of the sesame seeds and the mirin to make a rough paste. Wash the salmon. Grill (broil) the salmon and smoked mackerel under a high heat. Remove the skin and flake the fish. Keep the salmon and mackerel pieces separate. Toast the remaining sesame seeds.

2 Put a teacup and tablespoons into a bowl of water. Put salt into a dish. Wipe a board with a wet dish towel. Remove the teacup and shake off excess water. Scoop 30ml/2 tbsp rice into the cup. Make a well in the centre and add a quarter of the salmon. Cover with 15ml/1 tbsp rice. Press well.

3 Wet your hands, then spread a little salt over your palms. Turn the rice in the teacup out into one hand and squeeze to make a dense, flat ball. Wrap the ball with a nori strip. Put on the board. Make three more, then make four balls using the mackerel and another four using the umeboshi paste.

4 Scoop about 45ml/3 tbsp rice into the teacup. Mix in a quarter of the olives. Press the rice with your fingers. Wet your hands with water and rub with salt and a quarter of the toasted sesame seeds. Turn the teacup on to one hand and shape the rice into a ball. This time, do not wrap with nori. Repeat, making three more. Serve one kind of each ball on a plate with Japanese pickles.

Nutritional information per portion: Energy 548kcal/2288kJ; Protein 15.4g; Carbohydrate 90.8g, of which sugars 1g; Fat 13g, of which saturates 2.1g; Cholesterol 19mg; Calcium 108mg; Fibre 1.3g; Sodium 243mg.

Compressed sushi with smoked salmon

This sushi, known as Oshi-zushi, dates back almost a thousand years. The earliest forms of sushi were made as a means of preserving fish. The cooked rice produced an acid that preserved the fish. Only the marinated fish was eaten and the rice was discarded.

MAKES ABOUT 12

175g/6oz smoked salmon, thickly sliced
15ml/1 tbsp sake
15ml/1 tbsp water
30ml/2 tbsp shoyu

1 quantity *su-meshi*
1 lemon, thinly sliced into
    6 x 3mm/$\frac{1}{8}$in rings, to garnish

1 Lay the smoked salmon on a chopping board and sprinkle with a mixture of the sake, water and shoyu. Leave for an hour, then wipe dry.

2 Wet a wooden Japanese sushi mould or line a 25 x 7.5 x 5cm/10 x 3 x 2in plastic container with a large sheet of clear film (plastic wrap), allowing the edges to hang over.

3 Spread half the smoked salmon to evenly cover the bottom of the mould or container. Add a quarter of the cooked rice and firmly press down with your hands dampened with rice vinegar until it is 1cm/$\frac{1}{2}$in thick. Add the rest of the salmon, and press the remaining rice on top.

4 Put the wet wooden lid on the mould, or cover the plastic container with the overhanging clear film. Place a weight, such as a heavy dinner plate, on top. Leave in a cool place overnight, or for at least 3 hours. If you keep it in the refrigerator, choose the least cool part.

5 Remove the compressed sushi from the mould or container and unwrap. Cut into 2cm/$\frac{3}{4}$in slices and serve on a Japanese lacquered tray or a large plate. Quarter the lemon rings. Garnish with two slices of lemon on top of each piece and serve.

Nutritional information per portion: Energy 68kcal/286kJ; Protein 4.7g; Carbohydrate 10.2g, of which sugars 0.2g; Fat 0.7g, of which saturates 0.1g; Cholesterol 5mg; Calcium 6mg; Fibre 0g; Sodium 452mg.

Brown rice and mushrooms in clear soup

This is a good and quick way of using up left-over rice. Short grain Japanese or Italian brown rice are best for this recipe.

SERVES 4

1 litre/1³⁄₄ pints/4 cups second dashi stock, or the same amount of water and 20ml/4 tsp dashi-no-moto
60ml/4 tbsp sake
5ml/1 tsp salt
60ml/4 tbsp shoyu
115g/4oz fresh shiitake mushrooms, thinly sliced
600g/1lb 6oz cooked brown rice
2 large (US extra large) eggs, beaten
30ml/2 tbsp chopped fresh chives

FOR THE GARNISH
15ml/1 tbsp sesame seeds
shichimi togarashi (seven-spice powder), optional

1 Mix the dashi stock, sake, salt and shoyu in a large pan. Bring to the boil, then add the sliced shiitake. Cook for 5 minutes over a medium heat.

2 Add the cooked rice and stir over a medium heat. Break up any large chunks, and thoroughly warm the rice.

3 Pour the eggs into the pan. Lower the heat and cover. Do not stir. Remove from the heat after 3 minutes and stand for 3 minutes more. Sprinkle in the chives. Serve garnished with sesame seeds and shichimi togarashi.

Nutritional information per portion: Energy 280kcal/1180kJ; Protein 8.4g; Carbohydrate 50g, of which sugars 2.4g; Fat 4.7g, of which saturates 1.3g; Cholesterol 95mg; Calcium 48mg; Fibre 2.1g; Sodium 1111mg.

Rice in green tea with salmon

This is a common Japanese snack to have after drinks. In the Kyoto region, offering this dish used to be a way of saying the party was over.

SERVES 4

150g/5oz salmon fillet
¹⁄₄ nori sheet
250g/9oz/1¹⁄₄ cups Japanese short grain rice cooked using 350ml/12fl oz/1¹⁄₂ cups water
15ml/1 tbsp sencha leaves
5ml/1 tsp wasabi paste from a tube, or 5ml/1 tsp wasabi powder mixed with 1.5ml/¹⁄₄ tsp water (optional)
20ml/4 tsp shoyu
salt

1 Salt the salmon and leave for 30 minutes. Wipe off the salt and grill (broil) for 5 minutes until cooked through. Remove the skin and bones, then flake the salmon.

2 Cut the nori into narrow strips. If the rice is warm, put equal amounts into individual bowls. If the rice is cold, put in a sieve and pour hot water over it to warm it up. Drain and pour into the bowls. Place the salmon on top.

3 Put the sencha leaves in a teapot. Pour 600ml/1 pint/2¹⁄₂ cups hot water into the teapot and wait for 45 seconds. Strain the tea gently and evenly over the top of the rice and salmon. Add some nori and wasabi, if using, to the top of the rice, then trickle shoyu over and serve.

Nutritional information per portion: Energy 296kcal/1238kJ; Protein 12.5g; Carbohydrate 50.7g, of which sugars 0.7g; Fat 4.5g, of which saturates 0.7g; Cholesterol 19mg; Calcium 22mg; Fibre 0g; Sodium 729mg.

Miso soup

Essential to any Japanese meal is a bowl of rice. Next is miso soup, served in a lacquered bowl.
Of the many variations, Wakame To Tofu No Miso-shiru comes first.

SERVES 4

5g/¹/₈oz dried wakame
¹/₂ x 225–285g/8–10¹/₄oz packet fresh
    soft tofu or long-life silken tofu
400ml/14fl oz/1²/₃ cups second dashi
    stock or the same amount of water
    and 5ml/1 tsp dashi-no-moto
45ml/3 tbsp miso
2 spring onions (scallions), finely chopped
shichimi togarashi or sansho (optional),
    to serve

1 Soak the wakame in a large bowl
of cold water for 15 minutes.

2 Drain the wakame and chop into
stamp-size pieces if using the long
or broad type.

3 Cut the tofu into 1cm/¹/₂in strips,
then cut horizontally through the
strips. Cut the strips into squares.

4 Bring the dashi stock to the boil in
a medium saucepan.

5 Put the miso in a cup and mix
with 60ml/4 tbsp hot stock. Reduce
the heat and pour two-thirds of the
miso into the pan of stock.

6 Taste the soup and add more miso
if required. Add the wakame and
tofu and increase the heat. Just
before the soup comes to the boil
again, add the spring onions and
remove from the heat. Do not boil.
Serve sprinkled with shichimi
togarashi or sansho, if liked.

Nutritional information per portion: Energy 89kcal/371kJ; Protein 12.1g; Carbohydrate 1.9g, of which sugars 1.7g;
Fat 3.7g, of which saturates 1g; Cholesterol 32mg; Calcium 21mg; Fibre 0.6g; Sodium 1284mg.

Clear soup with seafood sticks

This delicate soup, called O-sumashi, which is often eaten with sushi, is very quick to make if you prepare the first dashi beforehand or if you use freeze-dried dashi-no-moto.

SERVES 4

4 mitsuba sprigs or 4 chives and a few
    sprigs of mustard and cress
4 seafood sticks
400ml/14fl oz/1²/₃ cups first dashi
    stock, or the same amount of water
    and 5ml/1 tsp dashi-no-moto
15ml/1 tbsp shoyu
7.5ml/1¹/₂ tsp salt
grated rind of yuzu (optional),
    to garnish

1 Cut off the root from the mitsuba, then cut 5cm/2in from the top, retaining both the long straw-like stem and the leaf.

2 Blanch the stems in hot water. If you use chives, choose those 10cm/4in in length and blanch them.

3 Take a seafood stick and carefully tie around the middle with a mitsuba stem or chive, holding it in place with a knot. Repeat to make four tied seafood sticks.

4 Loosen each end of a seafood stick to make it look like a tassel.

5 Place one seafood stick in each soup bowl. Add the four mitsuba leaves or mustard and cress.

6 Heat the dashi stock in a medium-sized pan and bring to the boil. Add shoyu and salt to taste. Pour the stock gently over the mitsuba and seafood stick. Sprinkle with grated yuzu rind, if using, and serve immediately.

Nutritional information per portion: Energy 30kcal/125kJ; Protein 5.4g; Carbohydrate 1g, of which sugars 0.9g; Fat 0.5g, of which saturates 0.1g; Cholesterol 23mg; Calcium 36mg; Fibre 0.2g; Sodium 877mg.

New Year's soup

The elaborate New Year's Day celebration brunch starts with a tiny glass of spiced warm sake, o-toso. Then, this New Year's soup, O-zoni, and other festive dishes are served.

SERVES 4

4 dried shiitake mushrooms
300g/11oz chicken thighs, bones
removed and reserved
300g/11oz salmon fillet, skin on, scaled
30ml/2 tbsp sake
50g/2oz satoimo or Jerusalem artichokes,
peeled
50g/2oz daikon, peeled
50g/2oz carrots, peeled

4 spring onions (scallions), white part
only, trimmed
4 mitsuba sprigs, root part removed
1 yuzu or lime
4 large raw tiger prawns (jumbo shrimp),
peeled, but with tails left on
30ml/2 tbsp shoyu
8 mochi (rice cake) slices
salt

1 Soak the dried shiitake overnight in 1 litre/1¾ pints/4 cups cold water. Remove the shiitake and pour the water into a pan. Bring to the boil, add the chicken bones, then reduce the heat to medium. Skim to remove scum. After 20 minutes, reduce the heat and simmer for 30 minutes until the liquid has reduced by a third. Strain into another pan.

2 Chop the chicken and salmon into small bitesize cubes. Par-boil in boiling water with 15ml/1 tbsp sake for 1 minute. Drain and wash.

3 Put the peeled satoimo in a pan and add enough water to cover. Add a pinch of salt and bring to the boil. Reduce the heat to medium, cook the satoimo for 15 minutes and drain.

4 Rinse and wipe the satoimo. Cut the satoimo, daikon and carrots into 1cm/½in cubes.

5 Discard the stalks from the shiitake, and slice the caps thinly. Chop the white part of the spring onions into 2.5cm/1in lengths.

6 Put the mitsuba into a sieve and pour hot water over them. Divide the leaves and stalk. Take a stalk and fold it into two and tie it in the middle to make a bow. Make four.

7 Cut the yuzu into four 3mm/⅛in thick round slices. Hollow out the inside to make rings. Add the remaining sake to the soup stock and bring to the boil. Add the daikon, carrot and shiitake, then reduce the heat to medium and cook for 15 minutes.

8 Put the prawns, satoimo or artichokes, spring onions, chicken and salmon into the pan. Wait for 5 minutes, then add the shoyu. Reduce the heat to low.

9 Cut the mochi in half crossways. Toast under a moderate preheated grill (broiler). Turn every minute until both sides are golden and the pieces have started to swell like a balloon; this will take about 5 minutes.

10 Quickly place the toasted mochi in individual soup bowls and pour the hot soup over the top. Arrange a mitsuba leaf in the centre of each bowl, put a yuzu or lime ring on top, and lay a mitsuba bow across. Serve immediately.

Nutritional information per portion: Energy 252kcal/1057kJ; Protein 36.4g; Carbohydrate 2.5g, of which sugars 2.3g; Fat 10.8g, of which saturates 2.1g; Cholesterol 165mg; Calcium 59mg; Fibre 1g; Sodium 857mg.

Miso soup with pork and vegetables

This is quite a rich and filling soup. Its Japanese name, Tanuki Jiru, *means raccoon soup for hunters, but as raccoons are not eaten nowadays, pork is used instead.*

SERVES 4

200g/7oz lean boneless pork
15cm/6in piece gobo or 1 parsnip
50g/2oz daikon
4 fresh shiitake mushrooms
1/2 konnyaku (yam cake) or 1/2 x
    225–285g/8–101/4oz packet tofu
a little sesame oil, for stir-frying

600ml/1 pint/21/2 cups of water and
    10ml/2 tsp dashi-no-moto
    (stock granules)
70ml/41/2 tbsp miso
2 spring onions (scallions), chopped
5ml/1 tsp sesame seeds

1 Press the meat down on a chopping board and slice horizontally into thin long strips. Cut the strips crossways into stamp-size pieces. Set aside.

2 Peel the gobo using a potato peeler, then cut diagonally into 1cm/1/2in thick slices. Quickly plunge the slices into a bowl of cold water to stop discolouring. If using parsnip, peel, cut in half lengthways, then cut into 1cm/1/2in thick half-moon-shaped slices. Peel and slice the daikon into 1.5cm/2/3in thick discs. Cut the discs into 1.5cm/2/3in cubes. Remove shiitake stalks and cut the caps into quarters.

3 Place the konnyaku in a pan of boiling water and cook for 1 minute. Drain and cool. Cut into quarters lengthways, then crossways into 3mm/1/8in thick pieces.

4 Heat a little sesame oil in a cast-iron pan until purple smoke rises. Stir-fry the pork, then add the tofu, if using, the konnyaku and all the vegetables except for the spring onions. When the colour of the meat has changed, add the stock. Bring to the boil over a medium heat and skim off the foam until the soups looks fairly clear. Reduce the heat, cover, and simmer for 15 minutes.

5 Put the miso in a bowl, and mix with 60ml/4 tbsp hot stock to make a smooth paste. Stir one-third of the miso into the soup. Add more miso to taste. Add the spring onion and remove from heat. Serve very hot in individual bowls sprinkled with sesame seeds.

Nutritional information per portion: Energy 89kcal/371kJ; Protein 12.1g; Carbohydrate 1.9g, of which sugars 1.7g; Fat 3.7g, of which saturates 1g; Cholesterol 32mg; Calcium 21mg; Fibre 0.6g; Sodium 1284mg.

Buckwheat noodles with dipping sauce

Cold soba noodles are often eaten in summer and served on a bamboo tray with a dipping sauce. The sauce enhances their flavour.

SERVES 4

4 spring onions (scallions), finely chopped
½ nori sheet, about 10cm/4in square
400g/14oz dried soba noodles
5ml/1 tsp wasabi paste from a tube, or
  5ml/1 tsp wasabi powder mixed with
  2.5ml/½ tsp water

FOR THE DIPPING SAUCE

30g/1¼oz kezuri-bushi
200ml/7fl oz/scant 1 cup shoyu
200ml/7fl oz/scant 1 cup mirin
750ml/1¼ pints/3 cups water

1 To make the dipping sauce, mix all the ingredients in a small pan. Bring to the boil, and cook for 2 minutes. Reduce the heat to medium, and cook for a further 2 minutes. Strain through muslin. Cool, then chill.

2 Soak the spring onions in ice-cold water in a bowl for 5 minutes. Drain and squeeze out the excess water. Toast the nori over a medium flame until dry and crisp, then cut it into short strips, 3mm/⅛in wide.

3 Heat 2 litres/3½ pints/9 cups water in a large pan. Bring to the boil, then add the soba. Distribute the noodles evenly in the pan, and stir to prevent sticking. When the water is bubbling, pour in 50ml/2fl oz/¼ cup cold water to lower the temperature. Repeat this process and cook according to the packet instructions, or about 5 minutes. To test if the noodles are ready, pick one out and cut it with your finger. It should be tender to the touch.

4 Put a large sieve under cold running water. Pour the cooked soba into the sieve, and wash with your hands. Rub the soba well to remove the starch; the soba should feel slightly elastic. Drain again.

5 Pour the dipping sauce into four cups. Put the wasabi and spring onions into individual dishes. Divide the soba among four plates or baskets. Sprinkle with nori strips and serve cold, with the sauce, wasabi and spring onions.

Nutritional information per portion: Energy 449kcal/1905kJ; Protein 12.1g; Carbohydrate 91.7g, of which sugars 17.9g; Fat 6.3g, of which saturates 0g; Cholesterol 0mg; Calcium 35mg; Fibre 3.1g; Sodium 360mg.

Soba noodles in hot soup with tempura

When you cook Japanese noodle dishes, everyone should be ready at the dinner table, because cooked noodles start to soften and lose their taste and texture quite quickly.

SERVES 4

400g/14oz dried soba noodles
1 spring onion (scallion), sliced
shichimi togarashi (optional)

FOR THE TEMPURA
16 medium raw tiger or king prawns
   (jumbo shrimp), heads and shell
   removed, tails intact
1 large (US extra large) egg, beaten
400ml/14fl oz/1²/₃ cups ice-cold water
200g/7oz/scant 2 cups plain
   (all-purpose) flour
vegetable oil, for deep-frying

FOR THE SOUP
150ml/¹/₄ pint/²/₃ cup mirin
150ml/¹/₄ pint/²/₃ cup shoyu
900ml/1¹/₂ pints/3³/₄ cups water
25g/1oz kezuri-bushi or 2 x 15g/¹/₂oz
   packets
15ml/1 tbsp caster (superfine) sugar
5ml/1 tsp salt
900ml/1¹/₂ pints/3³/₄ cups water and
   12.5ml/2¹/₂ tsp dashi-no-moto
   (stock granules)

1 To make the soup, put the mirin in a pan. Bring to the boil, then add the rest of the soup ingredients apart from the dashi. Bring back to the boil, then reduce the heat. Skim off the scum and simmer for 2 minutes. Strain the soup and put into a clean pan with the dashi stock.

2 Carefully remove the black vein from the prawns, then make 5 shallow cuts into each prawn's belly. Clip the tip of the tail and squeeze out any moisture.

3 To make the batter, mix the egg and water in a bowl. Sift in the flour and stir briefly; it should be fairly lumpy. Heat the oil in a wok to 180°C/350°F. Hold the tail of a prawn, dip it in the batter, then plunge it into the hot oil. Deep-fry two prawns at a time until crisp and golden. Drain on kitchen paper and keep warm.

4 Put the noodles in a large pan with at least 2 litres/3¹/₂ pints/9 cups rapidly boiling water, and stir frequently to stop them sticking. When the water foams, pour in 50ml/2floz/¹/₄ cup cold water to lower the temperature. Repeat when the water foams again. Transfer the noodles to a sieve and wash under cold water.

5 Heat the soup. Warm the noodles with hot water, and divide among serving bowls. Place the prawns on the noodles and add the soup.

6 Sprinkle each bowl with sliced spring onion and some shichimi togarashi, if you like.

Nutritional information per portion: Energy 794kcal/3356kJ; Protein 28g; Carbohydrate 135g, of which sugars 22.9g; Fat 19.5g, of which saturates 1.8g; Cholesterol 145mg; Calcium 155mg; Fibre 4.5g; Sodium 3278mg.

Udon noodles with egg broth and ginger

In this dish, called Ankake Udon, *the soup for the udon is thickened with cornflour and retains its heat for a long time. A perfect lunch for a freezing cold day.*

SERVES 4

400g/14oz dried udon noodles
30ml/2 tbsp cornflour (cornstarch)
4 eggs, beaten
50g/2oz mustard and cress
2 spring onions (scallions), finely chopped
2.5cm/1in fresh root ginger, peeled and
    finely grated, to garnish

FOR THE SOUP
1 litre/1³/4 pints/4 cups water
40g/1¹/2oz kezuri-bushi
25ml/1¹/2 tbsp mirin
25ml/1¹/2 tbsp shoyu
7.5ml/1¹/2 tsp salt

1 To make the soup, place the water and the soup ingredients in a pan and bring to the boil on a medium heat. Remove from the heat when it starts boiling. Stand for 1 minute, then strain through muslin (cheesecloth). Check the taste and add more salt if required.

2 Heat at least 2 litres/3¹/2 pints/9 cups water in a pan, and cook the udon for 8 minutes or according to the packet instructions. Drain under cold water and wash off the starch with your hands. Leave the udon in the sieve.

3 Pour the soup into a large pan and bring to the boil. Blend the cornflour with 60ml/4 tbsp water. Reduce the heat to medium and gradually add the cornflour mixture to the hot soup. Stir constantly. The soup will thicken after a few minutes. Reduce the heat to low.

4 Mix the egg, mustard, and cress, and spring onions in a bowl. Stir the soup again to create a whirlpool. Pour the eggs slowly into the soup pan. Reheat the udon with hot water. Divide among individual bowls and pour the soup over the top. Garnish with the ginger and serve hot.

Nutritional information per portion: Energy 517kcal/2187kJ; Protein 19.5g; Carbohydrate 87.7g, of which sugars 7g; Fat 12.4g, of which saturates 1.7g; Cholesterol 190mg; Calcium 130mg; Fibre 3.2g; Sodium 1019mg.

Pot-cooked udon in miso soup

Udon is a white wheat noodle, popular in the south and west of Japan. It is eaten with various hot and cold sauces and soups. Here, the noodles are cooked in a clay pot with a rich miso soup.

SERVES 4

200g/7oz chicken breast fillet,
   boned and skinned

10ml/2 tsp sake

2 abura-age

900ml/1¹/₂ pints/3³/₄ cups water
   and 7.5ml/1¹/₂ tsp dashi-no-moto
   (stock granules)

6 large fresh shiitake mushrooms, stalks
   removed, quartered

4 spring onions (scallions), trimmed and
   chopped into 3mm/¹/₈in lengths

30ml/2 tbsp mirin

about 90g/3¹/₂oz aka-miso or
   hatcho-miso

300g/11oz dried udon noodles

4 eggs

shichimi togarashi (optional)

1 Cut the chicken into bitesize pieces. Sprinkle with sake and leave to marinate for 15 minutes. Put the abura-age in a sieve and rinse with hot water. Drain on kitchen paper and cut each abura-age into four squares.

2 To make the soup, heat the water and stock granules in a large pan. When it has come to the boil, add the chicken, shiitake mushrooms and abura-age and cook for 5 minutes. Remove from the heat and add the spring onions.

3 Put the mirin and miso into a small bowl. Scoop 30ml/2 tbsp soup from the pan and mix this in well. To cook the udon, boil at least 2 litres/3¹/₂ pints/9 cups water in a large pan. Cook the udon for 6 minutes and drain.

4 Put the udon in a flameproof clay pot or casserole. Mix the miso paste into the soup and check the taste. Add more miso if required. Ladle in enough soup to cover the udon, and arrange the soup ingredients on top of the udon. Put the soup on a medium heat and break an egg on top. When the soup bubbles, wait for 1 minute, then cover and remove from the heat. Leave to stand for 2 minutes. Serve with shichimi togarashi, if you like.

Nutritional information per portion: Energy 439kcal/1855kJ; Protein 28.8g; Carbohydrate 59.5g, of which sugars 3.9g; Fat 11.1g, of which saturates 1.8g; Cholesterol 225mg; Calcium 59mg; Fibre 2.9g; Sodium 1707mg.

Cold somen noodles

At the height of summer, Hiya Somen – *cold somen noodles served immersed in cold water with ice cubes and accompanied by sauces and relishes – are a refreshing meal.*

SERVES 4

300g/11oz dried somen noodles

FOR THE DIPPING SAUCE
105ml/7 tbsp mirin
2.5ml/½ tsp salt
105ml/7 tbsp shoyu
20g/¾oz kezuri-bushi
400ml/14fl oz/1⅔ cups water

FOR THE RELISHES
2 spring onions (scallions), trimmed and
    finely chopped
2.5cm/1in fresh root ginger, peeled and
    finely grated

2 shiso leaves, finely chopped (optional)
30ml/2 tbsp toasted sesame seeds

FOR THE GARNISHES
10cm/4in cucumber
5ml/1 tsp salt
ice cubes or a block of ice
ice-cold water
115g/4oz cooked, peeled small prawns
    (shrimp)
orchid flowers or nasturtium flowers
    and leaves

1 To make the sauce, bring the mirin to the boil. Add the salt and shoyu and shake gently to mix. Add the kezuri-bushi and mix. Add the water and bring to the boil and cook for 3 minutes. Strain through muslin (cheesecloth) or a jelly bag. Cool, then chill for at least an hour before serving.

2 Prepare the garnish. Cut the cucumber in half and scoop out the seeds, then slice thinly. Sprinkle with the salt and leave for 20 minutes. Rinse in cold water and drain.

3 Bring at least 1.5 litres/2½ pints/6¼ cups water to the boil. Meanwhile, untie the bundle of somen. Have ready 75ml/2½fl oz/⅓ cup cold water. Put the somen in the boiling water. When it foams, pour the glass of water in. When the water boils again, the somen are ready. Drain into a colander under cold running water, and rub the somen with your hands to remove the starch. Drain.

4 Put some ice cubes in the centre of a chilled glass bowl, and add the somen. Pour on enough ice-cold water to cover the somen, then arrange cucumber slices, prawns and flowers on top. Prepare all the relishes separately in small dishes. Divide one-third of the sauce among four cups. Put the remaining sauce in a jug (pitcher). Serve the noodles cold with the relishes.

Nutritional information per portion: Energy 445kcal/1885kJ; Protein 16.3g; Carbohydrate 79.2g, of which sugars 23.7g; Fat 9.2g, of which saturates 0.7g; Cholesterol 56mg; Calcium 109mg; Fibre 2.9g; Sodium 2420mg.

Tokyo-style ramen noodles in soup

Ramen is a hybrid Chinese noodle dish presented in a Japanese way, and there are many different regional variations featuring local specialities. This dish is a legendary Tokyo version.

SERVES 4

250g/9oz dried ramen noodles

FOR THE SOUP STOCK
4 spring onions (scallions)
7.5cm/3in fresh root ginger, quartered
raw bones from 2 chickens, washed
1 large onion, quartered
4 garlic cloves, peeled
1 large carrot, roughly chopped
1 egg shell
120ml/4fl oz/¹⁄₂ cup sake
about 60ml/4 tbsp shoyu
2.5ml/¹⁄₂ tsp salt

**FOR THE *CHA-SHU*
(POT-ROAST PORK)**
500g/1¹⁄₄lb pork shoulder, boned
30ml/2 tbsp vegetable oil
2 spring onions (scallions), chopped
2.5cm/1in fresh root ginger, peeled and sliced
15ml/1 tbsp sake
45ml/3 tbsp shoyu
15ml/1 tbsp caster (superfine) sugar

FOR THE TOPPINGS
2 hard-boiled (hard-cooked) eggs
150g/5oz menma, soaked for 30 minutes and
    drained
¹⁄₂ nori sheet, broken into pieces
2 spring onions (scallions), chopped
ground white pepper
sesame oil or chilli oil

1 To make the soup stock, bruise the spring onions and ginger. Pour 1.5 litres/2¹⁄₂ pints/6¹⁄₄ cups water into a wok and bring to the boil. Add the chicken bones and boil until the colour of the meat changes. Discard the water and wash the bones.

2 Bring another 2 litres/3¹⁄₂ pints/9 cups water to the boil. Add the bones and other soup stock ingredients, except for the shoyu and salt. Reduce the heat and simmer until the water has reduced by half, skimming off any scum. Strain into a bowl through a muslin- (cheesecloth-) lined sieve.

3 Make the *cha-shu*. Roll the meat up tightly, 8cm/3¹⁄₂in in diameter, and tie with string. Heat the oil to smoking point in the wok and add the chopped spring onions and ginger. Cook briefly, then add the meat. Turn often to brown the outside evenly.

4 Sprinkle with sake and add 400ml/14fl oz/1²⁄₃ cups water, the shoyu and sugar. Boil, then reduce the heat to low and cover. Cook for 25–30 minutes, turning every 5 minutes. Remove from the heat.

5 Slice the pork into 12 fine slices. Shell and halve the boiled eggs, and sprinkle some salt according to taste on to the egg yolks to season.

6 Pour 1 litre/1¾ pints/4 cups soup stock from the bowl into a pan. Boil and add the shoyu and salt. Check the seasoning; add more shoyu if required.

7 Bring 2 litres/3½ pints/9 cups water to the boil. Cook the noodles according to their instructions. If the water bubbles, pour in 50ml/2fl oz/¼ cup cold water. Drain and divide among bowls.

8 Pour the soup over the noodles to cover. Arrange half a boiled egg, pork slices, menma and nori on top, and sprinkle with spring onions. Serve with pepper and sesame or chilli oil. Season to taste with a little salt, if you like.

Nutritional information per portion: Energy 359kcal/1503kJ; Protein 36.1g; Carbohydrate 19.8g, of which sugars 9.8g; Fat 15.4g, of which saturates 3.4g; Cholesterol 174mg; Calcium 248mg; Fibre 1.8g; Sodium 930mg.

Vegetable dishes

Because Japanese cooking is centred on

vegetables, preparation and cooking

techniques for them have been perfected

to achieve the best flavours and textures.

In this chapter, the inspiring combinations

of vegetables, mushrooms and seaweed

are typical of Japanese cooking. Although

the recipes are based on vegetables, many

also contain fish, chicken or meat.

Daikon and carrot salad

An essential dish for New Year celebrations, the bright colour combination of daikon and carrot is regarded as a symbol of happiness.

SERVES 4

20cm/8in daikon
2 carrots
5ml/1 tsp salt
45ml/3 tbsp caster (superfine) sugar
70ml/4½ tbsp rice vinegar
15ml/1 tbsp sesame seeds

1 Cut the daikon into three pieces, then thickly peel the skin. Peel the carrots and cut them into 5cm/2in pieces. Slice both vegetables thinly lengthways then crossways to make very thin matchsticks. Alternatively, shred them with a grater to achieve a similar effect.

2 Place the daikon and carrot in a bowl. Sprinkle with the salt and mix. Leave for 30 minutes, then drain and squeeze out the excess liquid. Transfer to another bowl.

3 Mix the sugar and vinegar together in a bowl. Stir until the sugar has dissolved. Pour over the daikon and carrot, and leave for at least a day, mixing two to three times.

4 To serve, mix the vegetables evenly and heap in the middle of a bowl. Sprinkle with sesame seeds and serve.

Nutritional information per portion: Energy 89kcal/373kJ; Protein 1.5g; Carbohydrate 16.2g, of which sugars 16g; Fat 2.5g, of which saturates 0.4g; Cholesterol 0mg; Calcium 55mg; Fibre 1.9g; Sodium 510mg.

Spinach with peanut sauce

Traditional Japanese cooking rarely uses fat or oil, and nuts have long been an important source of essential nutritional oils in the diet.

SERVES 4

450g/1lb spinach

FOR THE PEANUT SAUCE
50g/2oz/⅓ cup unsalted shelled peanuts
30ml/2 tbsp shoyu
7.5ml/1½ tsp caster (superfine) sugar
25ml/1½ tbsp second dashi stock, or the same amount of warm water with a pinch of dashi-no-moto

1 First, make the peanut sauce. Grind the shelled peanuts in a suribachi or a mortar and pestle. Alternatively, use an electric grinder.

2 Transfer the crushed nuts to a small mixing bowl and stir in the shoyu, sugar and dashi stock. When well mixed, the sauce will look like runny peanut butter.

3 Blanch the spinach for 30 seconds in rapidly boiling water until the leaves are wilted. Drain and cool under running water for 30 seconds.

4 Drain again and lightly squeeze out the excess water with your hands. Add the peanut sauce to the spinach in a bowl and mix gently. Serve on individual plates.

Nutritional information per portion: Energy 111kcal/460kJ; Protein 6.7g; Carbohydrate 6.3g, of which sugars 5.3g; Fat 6.7g, of which saturates 1.2g; Cholesterol 0mg; Calcium 202mg; Fibre 3.1g; Sodium 959mg.

Slow-cooked daikon

Freshly dug daikon is very juicy, and it is praised as the king of winter vegetables in Japan. In this dish, known as Furo Fuki Daikon, *the daikon is cooked slowly and served with tangy miso sauce.*

SERVES 4

1kg/2¼lb daikon, cut into 4 x 5cm/2in
    thick discs and peeled
15ml/1 tbsp rice (any kind except
    fragrant Thai or basmati)
100ml/3fl oz/scant ½ cup hatcho miso
60ml/4 tbsp caster (superfine) sugar
120ml/4fl oz/½ cup mirin
20cm/8in square dried konbu
rind of ¼ yuzu, shaved with a zester, to
    serve (optional)

1 Shave the top and bottom edge of each daikon section. Plunge into cold water. Drain and place flat in a pan. Pour in enough water to come 3cm/1¼in above the daikon. Add the rice and put on a high heat. When it comes to the boil, lower the heat and cook for 30 minutes.

2 Mix the miso and sugar in a pan. Add the mirin, a little at a time. Heat the mixture, stirring. When the mixture thickens, turn the heat to low. Cook, stirring, until the miso sauce sticks to a spoon. Remove from the heat and keep warm.

3 When the daikon is cooked, scoop the daikon, one by one, on to a flat-bottomed sieve and rinse with water. Discard the water and rice in the pan and wash the pan. Wipe the konbu with a wet cloth, and place in the pan. Add the daikon, just cover with water and warm for 15 minutes.

4 Divide the daikon among the bowls. Scoop out a little of the daikon at the top, then pour 15–20ml/3–4 tsp of the miso sauce over each piece. Garnish with yuzu zest, if using.

Nutritional information per portion: Energy 147kcal/622kJ; Protein 2.5g; Carbohydrate 34.9g, of which sugars 31.8g; Fat 0.5g, of which saturates 0.3g; Cholesterol 0mg; Calcium 64mg; Fibre 2.3g; Sodium 919mg.

Kabocha squash with chicken sauce

In this dish, known as **Kabocha Tori-soboro Kake,** *the mild sweetness of kabocha, similar to that of sweet potato, goes very well with the rich meat sauce.*

SERVES 4

1 kabocha squash, about 500g/1¼lb
½ yuzu or lime
20g/¾oz mangetouts (snow peas)
salt

FOR THE CHICKEN SAUCE
100ml/3fl oz/scant ½ cup water
30ml/2 tbsp sake
300g/11oz lean chicken, minced (ground)
60ml/4 tbsp caster (superfine) sugar
60ml/4 tbsp shoyu
60ml/4 tbsp mirin

1 Halve the kabocha squash, then remove the seeds and fibre around the seeds. Halve the squash again to make four wedges. Trim the stalky end of each kabocha wedge.

2 Remove strips of the peel on each of the wedges, cutting off strips lengthways of about 1–2.5cm/½–1in wide. Chop each wedge into large bitesize pieces. Place them side by side in a pan. Pour in enough water to cover, then sprinkle with salt. Cover and cook for 5 minutes over a medium heat, then lower the heat and simmer for 15 minutes until tender. Remove from the heat, cover and leave for 5 minutes.

3 Slice the yuzu or lime into thin discs, then hollow out the inside of the skin to make rings of peel. Cover with clear film (plastic wrap) until needed. Blanch the mangetouts in lightly salted water. Drain and set aside.

4 To make the sauce, bring the water and sake to the boil. Add the chicken, and when the meat is browned, add the sugar, shoyu and the mirin. Stir the mixture with a hand whisk until the liquid has almost all evaporated. Put the kabocha on a plate, then pour over the sauce. Add the mangetouts and garnish with yuzu rings.

Nutritional information per portion: Energy 172kcal/728kJ; Protein 19.6g; Carbohydrate 20g, of which sugars 19.2g; Fat 1.1g, of which saturates 0.4g; Cholesterol 53mg; Calcium 53mg; Fibre 1.4g; Sodium 1115mg.

Steamed aubergine with sesame sauce

This autumn recipe, Nasu Rikyu-ni, represents a typical Zen temple cooking style. Fresh seasonal vegetables are chosen and cooked with care. This dish is also delicious cold.

SERVES 4

2 large aubergines (eggplants)
400ml/14fl oz/1²/₃ cups second dashi stock, or the same amount of water with 5ml/ 1 tsp dashi-no-moto
25ml/1¹/₂ tbsp caster (superfine) sugar
15ml/1 tbsp shoyu
15ml/1 tbsp sesame seeds, finely ground in a suribachi or mortar and pestle
15ml/1 tbsp sake
15ml/1 tbsp cornflour (cornstarch)
salt

FOR THE ACCOMPANYING VEGETABLES

130g/4¹/₂oz shimeji mushrooms
115g/4oz/³/₄ cup fine green beans
100ml/3fl oz/scant ¹/₂ cup water with 5ml/1 tsp dashi-no-moto (stock granules)
25ml/1¹/₂ tbsp caster (superfine) sugar
15ml/1 tbsp sake
1.5ml/¹/₄ tsp salt
dash of shoyu

1 Peel the aubergines and cut in quarters lengthways. Prick all over with a skewer, then plunge into salted water for 30 minutes.

2 Drain and steam the aubergines in a steamer, or in a hot wok with a bamboo basket inside, for 20 minutes, or until soft.

3 Mix the dashi stock, sugar, shoyu and 1.5ml/¹/₄ tsp salt together in a pan. Transfer the aubergines to this pan, then cover and cook over a low heat for 15 minutes. Take a few tablespoonfuls of stock from the pan and mix with the ground sesame seeds. Add this mixture to the pan.

4 Mix the sake with the cornflour, add to the pan with the aubergines and stock and shake the pan gently, but quickly. When the sauce becomes quite thick, remove from the heat.

5 Prepare and cook the accompanying vegetables. Wash the mushrooms and cut off the hard base part. Separate the large block into smaller chunks. Trim the green beans and cut in half. Mix the stock with the sugar, sake, salt and shoyu in a shallow pan. Add the green beans and mushrooms and cook for 7 minutes until tender. Serve the aubergines with the accompanying vegetables.

Nutritional information per portion: Energy 79kcal/333kJ; Protein 2.9g; Carbohydrate 10.2g, of which sugars 9.6g; Fat 2.9g, of which saturates 0.5g; Cholesterol 0mg; Calcium 52mg; Fibre 3.3g; Sodium 272mg.

Carrot in sweet vinegar

In this refreshing side dish carrot strips are marinated in rice vinegar, shoyu and mirin. It makes a good accompaniment for oily foods.

SERVES 4

2 large carrots, peeled
5ml/1 tsp salt
30ml/2 tbsp sesame seeds

FOR THE SWEET VINEGAR MARINADE
75ml/5 tbsp rice vinegar
30ml/2 tbsp shoyu (use the pale awakuchi soy sauce if available)
45ml/3 tbsp mirin

1 Cut the carrots into thin matchsticks, 5cm/2in long. Put the carrots and salt into a bowl, and mix well. After 25 minutes, rinse the carrot in cold water, then drain.

2 In another bowl, mix together the marinade ingredients. Add the carrots, and marinate for 3 hours.

3 Put a small pan on a high heat, add the sesame seeds and toss constantly until the seeds start to pop. Remove from the heat and cool.

4 Chop the sesame seeds with a large, sharp knife on a large chopping board. Place the carrots in a bowl, sprinkle with the sesame seeds and serve cold.

Nutritional information per portion: Energy 110kcal/461kJ; Protein 2g; Carbohydrate 16.4g, of which sugars 16g; Fat 4.5g, of which saturates 0.7g; Cholesterol 0mg; Calcium 70mg; Fibre 1.8g; Sodium 1040mg.

Fried aubergine with miso sauce

Make sure the oil is smoking hot when adding the aubergine slices, so that they do not absorb too much oil.

SERVES 4

2 large aubergines (eggplants)
1–2 dried red chillies
45ml/3 tbsp sake
45ml/3 tbsp mirin
45ml/3 tbsp caster (superfine) sugar
30ml/2 tbsp shoyu
45ml/3 tbsp red miso (use either the dark red aka-miso or even darker hatcho-miso)
90ml/6 tbsp sesame oil
salt

1 Cut the aubergines into bitesize pieces and place in a colander, sprinkle with salt and leave for 30 minutes, then squeeze. Remove the seeds from the chillies and chop the chillies into rings.

2 Mix the sake, mirin, sugar and shoyu in a cup. In a separate bowl, mix the red miso with 45ml/3 tbsp water to make a loose paste.

3 Heat the oil in a large pan and add the chilli. When you see smoke, add the aubergine, and, using cooking hashi, stir-fry for 8 minutes until tender. Lower the heat.

4 Add the sake mixture, and stir for 2–3 minutes. If the sauce starts to burn, lower the heat. Add the miso paste to the pan and cook, stirring, for 2 minutes. Serve hot.

Nutritional information per portion: Energy 221kcal/916kJ; Protein 1.4g; Carbohydrate 13.7g, of which sugars 13.4g; Fat 16.9g, of which saturates 2.5g; Cholesterol 0mg; Calcium 20mg; Fibre 2g; Sodium 805mg.

Vegetarian tempura

In the hot Japanese summer, Zen monks eat deep-fried vegetables to get over the fatigue of hard training. Although tempura preparation needs a little effort, the result is worth it.

SERVES 4

15ml/1 tbsp lemon juice or rice vinegar

15cm/6in renkon, sliced

1/2 each sweet potato and aubergine (eggplant)

vegetable oil and sesame oil, for frying

4 shiso leaves

1 green (bell) pepper, seeded and cut
 lengthways into 2.5cm/1in wide strips

1/8 kabocha squash, cut into 5mm/1/4in thick
 half-ring shapes

4 green beans, trimmed

4 fresh shiitake mushrooms

4 okra, trimmed

1 onion, sliced into 5mm/1/4in rings

FOR THE BATTER

200ml/7fl oz/scant 1 cup ice-cold water

1 large (US extra large) egg, beaten

90g/3 1/2oz/generous 3/4 cup sifted plain
 (all-purpose) flour, plus extra for dusting

2–3 ice cubes

FOR THE CONDIMENT

4cm/1 1/2in piece fresh root ginger, grated

450g/1lb daikon, grated

FOR THE DIPPING SAUCE

400ml/14fl oz/1 2/3 cups water with 10ml/2 tsp
 dashi-no-moto (stock granules)

100ml/3fl oz/scant 1/2 cup shoyu

100ml/3fl oz/scant 1/2 cup mirin

1 To make the dipping sauce, mix all the ingredients in a pan. Bring to the boil, then remove from the heat. Set aside.

2 Fill a bowl with water and add the lemon juice. Peel the renkon, then slice it and the sweet potato into 5mm/1/4in thick discs and plunge into the bowl to prevent discolouring. Before frying, drain and dry. Slice the aubergine horizontally into 5mm/1/4in thick slices, then halve them lengthways. Soak in cold water before frying. Drain and dry.

3 Line an egg cup with clear film (plastic wrap) and press 2.5ml/1/2 tsp grated ginger into the bottom, then put in 30ml/2 tbsp grated daikon. Press again and turn upside-down on to a small plate. Make four of these mounds.

4 To make the batter, pour the ice-cold water into a bowl, add the egg and mix. Add the flour and roughly fold in. Do not beat. The batter should be quite lumpy. Add the ice cubes. Add oil to come halfway up the depth of a wok or deep-fryer. Heat the oil until the temperature reaches 150°C/300°F.

5 Deep-fry the shiso leaves. Hold the stalk of one leaf in your hand and stroke the leaf across the surface of the batter mix, coating one side of the leaf. Slip it into the oil until it goes crisp and bright green. Leave to drain. Deep-fry the renkon and sweet potato in the same way.

6 Increase the temperature to 175°C/347°F. Lightly dust the rest of the vegetables with flour, dunk into the batter mix, then shake off the excess. Deep-fry two to three pieces at a time until crisp. Leave to drain.

7 Divide the dipping sauce among four bowls. Place with the condiment. Arrange the tempura on a large plate and serve.

Nutritional information per portion: Energy 432kcal/1803kJ; Protein 8.2g; Carbohydrate 47g, of which sugars 24.6g; Fat 24.8g, of which saturates 3.4g; Cholesterol 48mg; Calcium 147mg; Fibre 5.8g; Sodium 1827mg.

Bacon-rolled enokitake mushrooms

The Japanese name for this dish is Obimaki enoki: *an obi (belt or sash) is made from bacon and wrapped around enokitake mushrooms before grilling them.*

SERVES 4

450g/1lb fresh enokitake mushrooms
6 rindless smoked streaky (fatty) bacon
    rashers (strips)
4 lemon wedges and ground white
    pepper, to serve

1 Cut off the root part of each enokitake cluster 2cm/$\frac{3}{4}$in from the end. Do not separate the stems. Cut the rashers in half lengthways.

2 Divide the enokitake into 12 bunches. Take one bunch, then place the middle of the enokitake near the edge of one bacon rasher.

3 Roll up the bunch of enokitake in the bacon. Slide the bacon slightly upwards at each roll to cover 4cm/$1\frac{1}{2}$in of the enokitake. Secure with a cocktail stick (toothpick). Repeat to make 11 more rolls.

4 Preheat the grill (broiler) to high. Place the enokitake rolls on an oiled wire rack. Grill (broil) both sides until the bacon is crisp and the enokitake start to burn. This takes about 10–13 minutes.

5 Remove the enokitake rolls and place on a board. Using a fork and knife, chop each roll in half in the middle of the bacon belt. Arrange the top part of the enokitake roll standing upright, the bottom part lying down next to it. Serve with a wedge of lemon and a small heap of ground white pepper.

Nutritional information per portion: Energy 118kcal/490kJ; Protein 8g; Carbohydrate 0.5g, of which sugars 0.2g; Fat 9.4g, of which saturates 3.2g; Cholesterol 24mg; Calcium 9mg; Fibre 1.3g; Sodium 478mg.

Slow-cooked shiitake with shoyu

Shiitake cooked slowly are so rich and filling that some people call them "vegetarian steak".
This dish, known as Fukumé-ni, *is a useful and flavourful addition to other dishes.*

SERVES 4

20 dried shiitake mushrooms
45ml/3 tbsp vegetable oil
30ml/2 tbsp shoyu
25ml/1¹⁄₂ tbsp caster (superfine) sugar
15ml/1 tbsp toasted sesame oil

1 Start soaking the shiitake the day before. Put them in a bowl almost full of water. Cover the shiitake with a plate to stop them floating. Leave to soak overnight.

2 Measure 120ml/4fl oz/¹⁄₂ cup liquid from the bowl. Drain the shiitake into a sieve. Remove and discard the stalks.

3 Heat the oil in a wok or a large pan. Stir-fry the shiitake over a high heat for 5 minutes, stirring.

4 Reduce the heat to low, then add the measured liquid, the shoyu and sugar. Cook until there is almost no moisture left. Add the sesame oil. Leave to cool, then slice and arrange the shiitake on a large plate.

Nutritional information per portion: Energy 133kcal/553kJ; Protein 1.2g; Carbohydrate 7.4g, of which sugars 7.2g; Fat 11.2g, of which saturates 1.4g; Cholesterol 0mg; Calcium 8mg; Fibre 0.6g; Sodium 537mg.

New potatoes cooked in dashi stock

Nikkorogashi *is a simple yet scrumptious dish, involving little more than new season's potatoes and onion cooked in dashi stock. As the stock evaporates, the onion becomes meltingly soft and caramelized, making a wonderful sauce that coats the potatoes.*

SERVES 4

15ml/1 tbsp toasted sesame oil
1 small onion, thinly sliced
1kg/2¼lb baby new potatoes, unpeeled

200ml/7fl oz/scant 1 cup second dashi
   stock, or the same amount of water
   with 5ml/1 tsp dashi-no-moto
45ml/3 tbsp shoyu

1 Heat the sesame oil in a wok or large pan. Add the onion slices and stir-fry for 30 seconds, then add the potatoes. Stir constantly, using cooking hashi for ease, until all the potatoes are well coated in sesame oil.

2 Pour on the dashi stock and shoyu and reduce the heat to the lowest setting. Cover and cook for 15 minutes, turning the potatoes every 5 minutes so they are evenly cooked.

3 Uncover the wok or pan for a further 5 minutes to reduce the liquid. If there is already very little liquid remaining, remove the wok or pan from the heat, cover and leave to stand for 5 minutes. Check that the potatoes are cooked, then remove from the heat.

4 Transfer the potatoes and onions to a deep serving bowl. Pour the sauce over the top and serve the dish immediately.

Nutritional information per portion: Energy 210kcal/890kJ; Protein 4.8g; Carbohydrate 42.4g, of which sugars 4.9g; Fat 3.5g, of which saturates 0.7g; Cholesterol 0mg; Calcium 21mg; Fibre 2.7g; Sodium 829mg.

Deep-fried layered shiitake and scallops

In this dish, you can taste three kinds of softness: chewy shiitake, mashed naga-imo with miso, and succulent scallop. The mixture creates a moment of heaven in your mouth. If it's difficult to eat with chopsticks, feel free to use a knife and fork.

SERVES 4

4 scallops

8 large fresh shiitake mushrooms

225g/8oz naga-imo, unpeeled

20ml/4 tsp miso

50g/2oz/1 cup fresh breadcrumbs

cornflour (cornstarch), for dusting

vegetable oil, for deep-frying

2 eggs, beaten

salt

4 lemon wedges, to serve

1 Slice the scallops in two horizontally, then sprinkle with salt. Remove the stalks from the shiitake by cutting them off with a knife. Discard the stalks. Cut slits on the top of the shiitake to form a white cross. Sprinkle with salt.

2 Heat a steamer and steam the naga-imo for 10–15 minutes, or until soft. Test with a skewer. Leave to cool. Wait until the naga-imo is cool enough to handle. Skin, then mash the flesh in a bowl. Add the miso and mix well. Break the breadcrumbs down finely. Mix half into the mashed naga-imo, keeping the rest on a small plate.

3 Fill the underneath of the shiitake caps with a scoop of mashed naga-imo. Smooth down with the flat edge of a knife and dust the mash with cornflour. Add a little mash to a slice of scallop and place on top. Spread another 5ml/1 tsp mashed naga-imo on to the scallop and shape to cover. Repeat to make eight little mounds.

4 Heat the oil to 150°C/300°F. Place the beaten eggs in a shallow container. Dust the shiitake and scallop mounds with cornflour, then dip into the egg. Handle with care as the mash and scallop are quite soft. Coat well with the remaining breadcrumbs and deep-fry in the oil until golden. Drain well on kitchen paper. Serve hot on individual plates with a wedge of lemon.

Nutritional information per portion: Energy 221kcal/918kJ; Protein 11.2g; Carbohydrate 11.7g, of which sugars 1.5g; Fat 14.6g, of which saturates 2.3g; Cholesterol 107mg; Calcium 50mg; Fibre 1.1g; Sodium 183mg.

Beans, tofu and eggs

The virtues of tofu as a nutrient could fill

a book, and the uses of this wonder food

are limitless. Tofu's essential blandness

adapts to and absorbs a host of other

flavours. Beans and eggs are equally

versatile and are perfect for making even

the simplest of dishes healthy and filling.

Cooked black-eyed beans

Traditionally, this dish was served in the coldest time of the year using only preserved food such as salted salmon and dried vegetables. Here, fresh salmon and vegetables are used instead.

SERVES 4

150g/5oz salmon fillet, boned and
   skinned
400g/14oz can black-eyed beans (peas)
   in brine
50g/2oz fresh shiitake mushrooms, stalks
   removed
50g/2oz carrot, peeled
50g/2oz daikon, peeled
5g/1/8oz dashi-konbu about 10cm/4in
   square
60ml/4 tbsp water
5ml/1 tsp caster (superfine) sugar
15ml/1 tbsp shoyu
7.5ml/1 1/2 tsp mirin
salt
2.5cm/1in fresh root ginger, peeled and
   thinly sliced or grated, to garnish

1 Slice the salmon into 1cm/1/2in thick pieces. Salt the fillet and leave for 1 hour, then wash away the salt and cut it into 1cm/1/2in cubes.

2 Par-boil the fish in boiling water for 30 seconds, then drain and wash.

3 Slice the fresh ginger thinly lengthways, then stack the slices and cut into thin threads. Soak for 30 minutes, then drain well.

4 Drain the can of beans and tip the liquid into a medium pan. Set the beans and liquid aside.

5 Chop all the vegetables into 1cm/1/2in cubes. Wipe the dried konbu with a damp dish towel, then snip with scissors.

6 Add the salmon, vegetables and konbu to the bean liquid with the beans, water, sugar and 1.5ml/1/4 tsp salt. Bring to the boil. Reduce the heat. Simmer for 6 minutes or until the carrot is cooked. Add the shoyu.

7 Cook for 4 minutes. Add the mirin, then remove from the heat, mix and check the seasoning. Leave for 1 hour. Garnish with the ginger.

Nutritional information per portion: Energy 198kcal/834kJ; Protein 16.9g; Carbohydrate 22.8g, of which sugars 3.9g; Fat 5g, of which saturates 1g; Cholesterol 19mg; Calcium 37mg; Fibre 4.1g; Sodium 294mg.

Sweet azuki bean soup with mochi rice cake

Azuki beans are commonly used in traditional Japanese desserts. This sweet soup for winter is eaten between meals as a snack, but never after the meal as it is quite filling.

SERVES 4

130g/4¹/₂oz/²/₃ cup dried azuki beans
pinch of baking powder
130g/4¹/₂oz/scant ³/₄ cup caster (superfine) sugar
1.5ml/¹/₄ tsp salt
4 mochi

1 Soak the azuki beans overnight in 1 litre/1³/₄ pints/4 cups water. Pour the beans and soaking water into a large pan, then bring to the boil. Reduce the heat to medium-low. Add the baking powder. Cover and cook for about 30 minutes.

2 Add a further 1 litre/1³/₄ pints/ 4 cups water, and bring back to the boil. Reduce the heat to low, and cook for a further 30 minutes.

3 When the beans are ready, they should crush easily. If they are still hard, cook for another 20 minutes.

4 Divide the sugar into two. Add one half to the pan with the beans and stir. Cook for 3 minutes, then add the rest and wait for 3 minutes.

5 Add the salt and cook for another 3 minutes. Keep the soup warm.

6 Cut the mochi in half. Grill (broil) under a moderate heat until light golden brown and puffy. Turn several times.

7 Put two pieces of mochi into small bowls and pour the soup around them. Serve hot.

Nutritional information per portion: Energy 270kcal/1148kJ; Protein 12.4g; Carbohydrate 52g, of which sugars 35.1g; Fat 2.9g, of which saturates 0.5g; Cholesterol 0mg; Calcium 331mg; Fibre 2.7g; Sodium 10mg.

Stuffed and grilled thin tofu

In Japan, spring onions are thought to prevent colds, and this dish is made doubly effective by also including grated garlic.

SERVES 4

1 packet abura-age (2 abura-age per
   packet)

FOR THE FILLING
4 spring onions (scallions), trimmed
   and very finely chopped
about 15ml/1 tbsp shoyu
1 garlic clove, grated or crushed
30ml/2 tbsp lightly toasted sesame seeds

1 Put the abura-age in a sieve and pour hot water over to wash off excess oil. Drain and gently dry on kitchen paper.

2 Put one abura-age on a board and roll over several times with a rolling pin. Cut it in half and carefully open at the cut part to make two bags. Repeat the process with the remaining piece of abura-age.

3 Mix the spring onions, shoyu, garlic and sesame seeds in a small bowl. Check the seasoning and add more shoyu, if required.

4 Fill the bags with the filling. Grill (broil) for 3–4 minutes on each side until crisp and lightly browned.

5 Cut into four triangles and arrange on four small plates. Serve hot.

Nutritional information per portion: Energy 235kcal/976kJ; Protein 18.4g; Carbohydrate 2.1g, of which sugars 1.2g; Fat 17g, of which saturates 0.6g; Cholesterol 0mg; Calcium 1109mg; Fibre 0.8g; Sodium 278mg.

Deep-fried tofu in dashi soup

A creamy tofu block is deep-fried in a crisp thin batter, then soaked in hot broth. This tasty dish is typical in a Zen vegetarian menu.

SERVES 4

2 x 295g/10¾oz packets long-life soft
   or silken tofu, drained
vegetable oil, for deep-frying
30ml/2 tbsp plain (all-purpose) flour

FOR THE SAUCE
50ml/2fl oz/¼ cup shoyu
50ml/2fl oz/¼ cup mirin
pinch of salt
300ml/½ pint/1¼ cups second dashi
   stock, or the same amount of water
   and 7.5ml/1½ tsp dashi-no-moto

FOR THE GARNISH
2.5cm/1in fresh root ginger, peeled
   and finely grated
60ml/4 tbsp finely chopped chives

1 Wrap the tofu in 2–3 layers of kitchen paper. Set a chopping board, or large plate with a weight, on top to press the tofu, and leave for 30 minutes.

2 To make the sauce, place the shoyu, mirin, salt and dashi stock in a pan over a medium heat. Mix and cook for 5 minutes, then set aside.

3 Squeeze the ginger and make into four balls. Set aside. Unwrap the tofu and pat dry. Slice one tofu block into four squares each 2.5 x 6cm/1 x 2½in. Repeat with the other tofu block.

4 Heat the oil to 190°C/375°F. Dust the tofu with the flour and slide into the oil. Deep-fry until golden. Drain well on kitchen paper.

5 Arrange two tofu pieces in each bowl. Reheat the sauce and pour from the side of the bowl. Put a ginger ball on the tofu and sprinkle with chives. Serve.

Nutritional information per portion: Energy 40kcal/164kJ; Protein 3.9g; Carbohydrate 1.1g, of which sugars 0.9g; Fat 2.2g, of which saturates 0.4g; Cholesterol 24mg; Calcium 187mg; Fibre 0.3g; Sodium 380mg.

Deep-fried tofu balls

There are many variations of these delicious deep-fried tofu balls called hiryozu, *meaning flying dragon's head. This is one of the easiest to make.*

MAKES 16

2 x 285g/10¼oz packets tofu blocks
20g/³⁄₄oz carrot, peeled
40g/1½oz/1¼ cups green beans
2 large (US extra large) eggs, beaten
30ml/2 tbsp sake
10ml/2 tsp mirin
5ml/1 tsp salt
10ml/2 tsp shoyu
pinch of caster (superfine) sugar
vegetable oil, for deep-frying
4 chives, finely snipped, to garnish

FOR THE LIME SAUCE

45ml/3 tbsp shoyu
juice of ½ lime
5ml/1 tsp rice vinegar

TO SERVE

175g/6oz daikon, peeled
2 dried red chillies, halved and seeded

1 Drain the tofu and wrap in a clean dish towel. Set a plate with a weight on top and leave for 2 hours, or until the tofu loses most of its liquid.

2 Cut the daikon into thick slices. Make 3 holes in each slice and insert chilli pieces into the holes. Leave for 15 minutes, then grate.

3 To make the tofu balls, chop the carrot finely. Slice the beans finely. Cook both vegetables for 1 minute.

4 In a food processor, mix the tofu, eggs, sake, mirin, salt, shoyu and sugar until smooth.

5 Transfer the mixture to a bowl and mix in the carrot and beans. Fill a wok with oil 4cm/1½in deep, and heat to 185°C/365°F.

6 Wet your hands with a little oil. Shape 40ml/8 tsp tofu mixture into a ball. Deep-fry until crisp and golden and drain. Repeat with the remaining mixture. Sprinkle the tofu balls with chives. Put 30ml/2 tbsp grated daikon and chillies in each of four small bowls.

7 Mix the lime sauce ingredients in a serving bowl. Serve the balls with the lime sauce and grated daikon.

Nutritional information per portion: Energy 40kcal/164kJ; Protein 3.9g; Carbohydrate 1.1g, of which sugars 0.9g; Fat 2.2g, of which saturates 0.4g; Cholesterol 24mg; Calcium 187mg; Fibre 0.3g; Sodium 380mg.

Pan-fried tofu with caramelized sauce

Tofu in the West is often used as a meat substitute for vegetarians, as it was by Chinese Buddhist monks who first brought vegetarian cooking into Japan. They invented many delicious dishes.

SERVES 4

2 x 285g/10¼oz packets tofu blocks, drained
4 garlic cloves
10ml/2 tsp vegetable oil
50g/2oz/¼ cup butter, cut into 5 equal pieces
watercress, to garnish

FOR THE MARINADE

4 spring onions (scallions), finely chopped
60ml/4 tbsp sake
60ml/4 tbsp shoyu (tamari or sashimi soy sauce, if available)
60ml/4 tbsp mirin

1 Wrap the tofu in three layers of kitchen paper. Put a board on top as a weight and leave for 30 minutes.

2 Mix all the marinade ingredients and leave for 15 minutes.

3 Slice the garlic thinly. Heat the oil in a frying pan and fry the garlic until golden. Turn frequently to prevent sticking and burning. Scoop them out on to kitchen paper. Reserve the oil in the pan.

4 Slice the tofu blocks horizontally in half, then cut each half into four pieces. Soak in the marinade for 15 minutes. Wipe off excess marinade Reserve the marinade.

5 Reheat the oil in the pan and add a piece of butter. When the oil starts sizzling, reduce the heat and add the tofu one by one. Cover and cook for about 5–8 minutes on each side.

6 Cook the marinade for 2 minutes. Arrange four pieces of tofu on each plate. Pour over the marinade mixture and top with butter. Sprinkle with garlic chips and garnish with watercress.

Nutritional information per portion: Energy 271kcal/1127kJ; Protein 12.7g; Carbohydrate 11.5g, of which sugars 10g; Fat 17.9g, of which saturates 7.4g; Cholesterol 27mg; Calcium 742mg; Fibre 0.4g; Sodium 1152mg.

Grilled vegetable sticks

For this tasty kebab-style dish, made with tofu, konnyaku and aubergine, you will need 40 bamboo skewers, soaked in water overnight to prevent them burning when grilled.

SERVES 4

1 x 285g/10¼oz packet tofu block
1 x 250g/9oz packet konnyaku
2 small aubergines (eggplants)
25ml/1½ tbsp toasted sesame oil

FOR THE YELLOW AND GREEN SAUCES
45ml/3 tbsp shiro-miso
15ml/1 tbsp caster (superfine) sugar
5 young spinach leaves
2.5ml/½ tsp sansho
salt

FOR THE RED SAUCE
15ml/1 tbsp aka-miso
5ml/1 tsp caster (superfine) sugar
5ml/1 tsp mirin

TO GARNISH
pinch of white poppy seeds
15ml/1 tbsp toasted sesame seeds

1 Drain the liquid from the tofu packet and wrap the tofu in three layers of kitchen paper. Set a chopping board on top to press out the remaining liquid. Leave for 30 minutes until the excess liquid has been absorbed by the kitchen paper. Cut into eight 7.5 x 2 x 1cm/3 x ¾ x ½in slices.

2 Drain the liquid from the konnyaku. Cut it in half and put in a small pan with enough water to cover. Bring to the boil and cook for about 5 minutes. Drain and cut it into eight 6 x 2 x 1cm/2½ x ¾ x ½in slices.

3 Cut the aubergines into two lengthways, then halve the thickness to make four flat slices. Soak in cold water for 15 minutes. Drain and pat dry. To make the yellow sauce, mix the shiro-miso and sugar in a pan, then cook over a low heat, stirring to dissolve the sugar. Remove from the heat. Place half the sauce in a small bowl.

4 Blanch the spinach leaves in rapidly boiling water with a pinch of salt for 30 seconds and drain, then cool under running water. Squeeze out the water and chop finely. Transfer to a mortar and pound to a paste using a pestle. Mix the paste and sansho pepper into the bowl of yellow sauce to make the green sauce.

5 Put all the red sauce ingredients in a small pan and cook over a low heat, stirring constantly, until the sugar has dissolved. Remove from the heat.

6 Pierce the slices of tofu, konnyaku and aubergine with two bamboo skewers each. Heat the grill (broiler) to high. Brush the aubergine slices with sesame oil and grill (broil) for 7–8 minutes each side. Turn several times.

7 Grill the konnyaku and tofu slices for 3–5 minutes each side, or until lightly browned. Remove them from the heat but keep the grill hot.

8 Spread the red miso sauce on the aubergine slices. Spread one side of the tofu slices with green sauce and one side of the konnyaku with the yellow miso sauce from the pan. Grill the slices for 1–2 minutes. Sprinkle the aubergines with poppy seeds. Sprinkle the konnyaku with sesame seeds and serve all together.

Nutritional information per portion: Energy 178kcal/742kJ; Protein 12.9g; Carbohydrate 9.3g, of which sugars 8.6g; Fat 10.2g, of which saturates 1.4g; Cholesterol 0mg; Calcium 761mg; Fibre 1.9g; Sodium 17mg.

Simmered tofu with vegetables

A typical Japanese dinner at home consists of a soup, three different dishes and a bowl of rice. One of the three dishes is always a simmered one like this.

SERVES 4

4 dried shiitake mushrooms

450g/1lb daikon, peeled

2 atsu-age, about 200g/7oz each

115g/4oz/³⁄₄ cup green beans, trimmed
   and cut in half

5ml/1 tsp rice (any except for fragrant
   Thai or white basmati)

115g/4oz carrot, peeled and cut into
   1cm/¹⁄₂in thick slices

300g/11oz baby potatoes, unpeeled

750ml/1¹⁄₄ pints/3 cups water and
   7.5ml/1¹⁄₂ tsp dashi-no-moto
   (stock granules)

30ml/2 tbsp caster (superfine) sugar

75ml/5 tbsp shoyu

45ml/3 tbsp sake

15ml/1 tbsp mirin

1 Soak the dried shiitake in 250ml/8fl oz/1 cup water for 2 hours. Drain and discard the liquid. Remove and discard the stalks. Slice the daikon into 1cm/¹⁄₂in discs. Shave the edge of the daikon discs to ensure they are evenly cooked. Plunge into cold water.

2 Put the atsu-age in a sieve, and wash off the excess oil with hot water. Drain and cut into pieces of about 2.5 x 5cm/1 x 2in. Boil the green beans for 2 minutes, then drain and cool. Cover the daikon with water in a pan and add the rice. Bring to the boil then reduce the heat to medium-low. Cook for 15 minutes, then drain. Discard the rice.

3 Put the atsu-age, mushrooms, carrot and potatoes into the pan with the daikon. Add the dashi, bring to the boil, then reduce the heat. Skim off any scum. Add the sugar, shoyu and sake, shaking the pan to mix thoroughly.

4 Cut baking parchment into a circle 1cm/¹⁄₂in smaller than the pan lid and place inside the pan. Cover with the lid and simmer for 30 minutes, or until the sauce has reduced by half. Add the green beans for 2 minutes so that they just warm through.

5 Remove the paper and add the mirin. Taste the sauce and adjust with shoyu if required. Remove from the heat. Arrange the ingredients on a serving plate. Pour over a little sauce, and serve warm or cold.

Nutritional information per portion: Energy 142kcal/597kJ; Protein 4.2g; Carbohydrate 27.6g, of which sugars 15.1g; Fat 0.9g, of which saturates 0.3g; Cholesterol 0mg; Calcium 92mg; Fibre 3.3g; Sodium 1406mg.

Savoury egg soup

This delicious custard-like soup is softer and runnier than a Western custard pudding. It contains tasty surprises, such as pink prawns and jade-green gingko nuts.

SERVES 4

8 gingko nuts, shelled (or canned)

4 medium raw tiger prawns (jumbo shrimp), peeled, heads and tails removed, and deveined

5cm/2in carrot, thinly sliced

4 mitsuba sprigs

75g/3oz chicken breast fillet, skinned

5ml/1 tsp sake

5ml/1 tsp shoyu

2 fresh shiitake mushrooms, thinly sliced, stalks discarded

salt

FOR THE CUSTARD

3 large (US extra large) eggs, beaten

500ml/17fl oz/generous 2 cups water and 2.5ml/¹⁄₂ tsp dashi-no-moto (stock granules)

15ml/1 tbsp sake

15ml/1 tbsp shoyu

2.5ml/¹⁄₂ tsp salt

1 Boil the gingko nuts for 5 minutes. Drain. Remove any skin. Blanch the prawns in hot water until they curl up. Drain and pat dry. Cut the carrot slices into maple-leaf shapes. Blanch and drain.

2 Cut off the mitsuba roots. Cut the stems 2.5cm/1in from the top and keep the leaves. Halve the stems and wilt in hot water. Tie two mitsuba stems together.

3 Dice the chicken, then marinate in the sake and shoyu for 15 minutes.

4 To make the custard, put all the ingredients in a bowl. Mix and strain into another bowl. Bring a steamer to the boil, then lower the heat.

5 Divide the chicken, shiitake, gingko nuts, prawns and carrots among four ramekins. Divide the egg mixture among the ramekins.

6 Put the mitsuba stems on top, and the leaves if you like, and then cover each ramekin with a piece of foil. Place them in the steamer on low for 15 minutes until set. Serve hot.

Nutritional information per portion: Energy 163kcal/681kJ; Protein 16g; Carbohydrate 2.4g, of which sugars 1g; Fat 9.7g, of which saturates 2.3g; Cholesterol 205mg; Calcium 48mg; Fibre 0.5g; Sodium 654mg.

Rolled omelette

Easier to make than it looks, all that is needed to make this light and sweet omelette is a sushi rolling mat, wrapped in clear film. Use a round or rectangular frying pan.

SERVES 4

45ml/3 tbsp second dashi stock, or the
    same amount of water and a pinch
    of dashi-no-moto
30ml/2 tbsp mirin
15ml/1 tbsp caster (superfine) sugar
5ml/1 tsp shoyu
5ml/1 tsp salt
6 large (US extra large) eggs, beaten
vegetable oil

FOR THE GARNISH
2.5cm/1in daikon
4 shiso leaves (optional)
shoyu

1 Warm the stock. Mix in the mirin, sugar, shoyu and salt. Add to the eggs and stir well. Heat an omelette pan over medium heat. Soak kitchen paper in oil and wipe the pan.

2 Pour in a quarter of the egg mixture and tilt the pan to coat it. When the egg starts to set, roll it up towards you with chopsticks.

3 Keeping the rolled omelette in the pan, push it away from you. Oil the empty part of the pan again. Pour one-third of the egg mixture in at the empty side. Lift up the first roll with chopsticks, so the egg mixture runs underneath. When half set, roll the omelette around the first roll.

4 Move the roll gently on to a sushi rolling mat covered with clear film (plastic wrap). Roll the omelette firmly into the roller mat. Stand for 5 minutes and repeat the process again to make another roll.

5 Grate the daikon with a grater. Squeeze out the juice.

6 Cut the rolled omelettes into 2.5cm/1in slices crossways.

7 Lay the shiso leaves, if using, on four small plates and place a few slices of the omelette on top. Put a small heap of grated daikon to one side and add a few drops of shoyu to the top.

Nutritional information per portion: Energy 205kcal/854kJ; Protein 9.5g; Carbohydrate 11.9g, of which sugars 11.9g; Fat 13.8g, of which saturates 3g; Cholesterol 285mg; Calcium 49mg; Fibre 0g; Sodium 686mg.

Fish and shellfish

There are numerous delicious fish dishes in the Japanese culinary tradition, including many using fish that is so fresh it does not require cooking. The very freshest shellfish and fish are used to make sashimi. Other favourite methods range from "cooking" the fresh fish in vinegar, to flavouring it with seaweed, or frying the fish in a batter to create the classic dish, tempura.

Seared swordfish with citrus dressing

Kajiki No Tataki Salad is a good example of how the Japanese adopt new dishes from all over the world. Fresh fish is sliced thinly and seared or marinated, then served with salad and vegetables.

SERVES 4

75g/3oz daikon, peeled
50g/2oz carrot, peeled
1 Japanese or salad cucumber
10ml/2 tsp vegetable oil
300g/11oz skinned fresh swordfish steak,
    cut against the grain
2 cartons mustard and cress
15ml/1 tbsp toasted sesame seeds

FOR THE DRESSING

105ml/7 tbsp shoyu
105ml/7 tbsp second dashi stock, or the
    same amount of water and 5ml/1 tsp
    dashi-no-moto
30ml/2 tbsp toasted sesame oil
juice of 1/2 lime
rind of 1/2 lime, shredded into thin strips

1 Make the vegetable garnishes first. Use a very sharp knife, mandolin or vegetable slicer with a julienne blade to make very thin (about 4cm/1½in long) strands of daikon, carrot and cucumber. Soak the daikon and carrot in ice-cold water for 5 minutes, then drain and chill.

2 Mix together all the ingredients for the dressing and stir, then chill.

3 Heat the oil in a frying pan until smoking hot. Sear the fish for 30 seconds on all sides. Plunge it into cold water to stop the cooking. Dry and wipe off as much oil as possible.

4 Cut the swordfish steak in half lengthways before slicing it into 5mm/¼in thick pieces in the other direction, against the grain.

5 Arrange the fish slices into a ring on individual plates.

6 Mix the vegetable strands, mustard and cress and sesame seeds together. Fluff up with your hands, then shape them into a sphere. Gently place it in the centre of the plate, on top of the swordfish.

7 Pour the dressing around the plate's edge and serve immediately.

Nutritional information per portion: Energy 223kcal/925kJ; Protein 15.4g; Carbohydrate 3.6g, of which sugars 3.3g; Fat 16.4g, of which saturates 2.5g; Cholesterol 31mg; Calcium 46mg; Fibre 0.9g; Sodium 1975mg.

Marinated salmon with avocado

Use only the freshest of salmon for this delicious salad. The marinade of lemon and dashi-konbu "cooks" the salmon, which is then served with avocado, almonds, salad and a miso mayonnaise.

SERVES 4

250g/9oz very fresh salmon tail, skinned and filleted
juice of 1 lemon
10cm/4in dashi-konbu, wiped with a damp cloth and cut into 4 strips
1 ripe avocado
4 shiso leaves, stalks removed and cut in half lengthways
about 115g/4oz mixed leaves such as lamb's lettuce, frisée or rocket (arugula)
45ml/3 tbsp flaked (sliced) almonds, toasted in a dry frying pan until just slightly browned

FOR THE MISO MAYONNAISE

90ml/6 tbsp good-quality mayonnaise
15ml/1 tbsp shiro-miso
ground black pepper

1 Cut the first salmon fillet in half crossways at the tail end where the fillet is not wider than 4cm/1½in. Next, cut the wider part in half lengthways. Cut the other fillet in the same way.

2 Pour the lemon juice and two of the dashi-konbu pieces into a wide plastic container. Lay the salmon fillets in the base and sprinkle with the rest of the dashi-konbu.

3 Marinate for 15 minutes, then turn once and leave for a further 15 minutes. The salmon should change to a pink "cooked" colour. Remove the salmon from the marinade and wipe with kitchen paper.

4 Cut the salmon into 5mm/¼in thick slices against the grain.

5 Halve the avocado and sprinkle with a little of the remaining marinade. Remove the avocado stone (pit) and skin, then slice to the same thickness as the salmon.

6 Mix the mayonnaise ingredients together. Spread 5ml/1 tsp on to the back of each of the shiso leaves, then mix the remainder with 15ml/1 tbsp of the marinade.

7 Arrange the salad on four plates. Top with the avocado, salmon, shiso leaves and almonds, and drizzle over the remaining miso mayonnaise.

Nutritional information per portion: Energy 422kcal/1745kJ; Protein 16g; Carbohydrate 2.1g, of which sugars 1.4g; Fat 38.9g, of which saturates 5.9g; Cholesterol 48mg; Calcium 53mg; Fibre 2g; Sodium 133mg.

Lemon sole and fresh oyster salad

Oysters, flavoured with a rice-vinegar dressing, taste wonderful with lemon sole sashimi. In Japan, there is no choice of fish on a menu – it depends on which fish was caught that day.

SERVES 4

1 very fresh lemon sole, skinned and
    filleted into 4 pieces
105ml/7 tbsp rice vinegar
dashi-konbu, in 4 pieces, big enough to
    cover the fillets
50g/2oz Japanese cucumber, trimmed,
    or salad cucumber with seeds removed
50g/2oz celery sticks, strings removed
450g/1lb large broad (fava) beans,
    podded
1 lime, ½ thinly sliced
60ml/4 tbsp walnut oil
seeds from ½ pomegranate
salt

FOR THE OYSTERS

15ml/1 tbsp rice vinegar
30ml/2 tbsp shoyu
15ml/1 tbsp sake
12 large fresh oysters, opened
25g/1oz daikon or radishes, peeled and
    very finely grated
8 chives

1 Sprinkle salt on the sole fillets. Cover and chill for an hour. Mix the rice vinegar and a similar amount of water in a bowl. Wash the fish fillets in the mixture, then drain. Cut each fillet in half lengthways.

2 Lay one piece of dashi-konbu on a work surface. Place a pair of sole fillets, skinned sides together, on to it, then lay another piece of konbu on top. Cover all the fillets like this and chill for 3 hours.

3 Halve the cucumber crossways and slice thinly lengthways. Slice diagonally into 2cm/¾in wide pieces. Repeat for the celery. Sprinkle the cucumber with salt and leave for 30–60 minutes. Squeeze to remove moisture. Boil the beans for 15 minutes. Drain, cool, then peel off the skins. Sprinkle with salt. Mix the vinegar, shoyu and sake in a bowl. Slice the sole thinly.

4 Place the cucumber and celery in a mound in the centre of four plates. Lay lime slices on top. Garnish with chives. Place the oysters to one side of the cucumber, topped with broad beans, then season with 5ml/1 tsp of the vinegar and 10ml/2 tsp grated daikon. Arrange the sole on the other side and drizzle with walnut oil and lime juice. Add the pomegranate seeds and serve.

Nutritional information per portion: Energy 264kcal/1105kJ; Protein 22.7g; Carbohydrate 14.8g, of which sugars 1.9g; Fat 13.1g, of which saturates 1.3g; Cholesterol 56mg; Calcium 143mg; Fibre 7.6g; Sodium 295mg.

Scallops sashimi in mustard sauce

The Japanese name, Hotate Kobachi, *means "scallop in a little deep bowl". This is a typical serving size for lots of Japanese dishes as a meal usually consists of at least three dishes or more.*

SERVES 4

8 scallops or 16 queen scallops, cleaned and coral removed
¼ dried sheet chrysanthemum petals (sold as kiku nori) or a handful of edible flower petals such as yellow nasturtium
4 bunches of watercress, leaves only

FOR THE DRESSING
30ml/2 tbsp shoyu
5ml/1 tsp sake
10ml/2 tsp English (hot) mustard

1 Slice the scallops in three horizontally then cut in half crossways. If you use queen scallops, slice in two horizontally.

2 Put the dried chrysanthemum or the flower petals in a sieve. Pour hot water from a kettle all over, and leave to drain for a while. When cool, gently squeeze the excess water out. Set aside and repeat with the watercress.

3 Mix together all the ingredients for the dressing in a bowl. Add the scallops 5 minutes before serving and mix well without breaking them. Add the flower petals and watercress, then transfer to four small bowls. Serve cold. Add a little more shoyu, if required.

COOK'S TIP
Do not use chrysanthemums from your garden, as the edible species are different to the ornamental varieties. Fresh edible chrysanthemums and other edible flowers are often available at specialist Japanese stores, or look for dried ones in Asian stores.

Nutritional information per portion: Energy 62kcal/262kJ; Protein 10.5g; Carbohydrate 2.5g, of which sugars 1g; Fat 1g, of which saturates 0.3g; Cholesterol 19mg; Calcium 58mg; Fibre 0.4g; Sodium 852mg.

Turbot sashimi salad with wasabi

Eating sashimi, or raw fish, with traditional sauces disappeared when shoyu became popular in the 17th century. The use of sauces returned with the Western-inspired salad.

SERVES 4

ice cubes
400g/14oz very fresh thick turbot,
    skinned and filleted
300g/11oz mixed salad leaves
8 radishes, thinly sliced

FOR THE WASABI DRESSING

25g/1oz rocket (arugula) leaves
50g/2oz cucumber, chopped
90ml/6 tbsp rice vinegar
75ml/5 tbsp olive oil
5ml/1 tsp salt
15ml/1 tbsp wasabi paste, or the same
    amount of wasabi powder mixed with
    7.5ml/1½ tsp water

1 For the dressing, roughly tear the rocket and mix with the cucumber and vinegar in a food processor. Pour into a bowl and add the rest of the dressing ingredients, except the wasabi. Check the seasoning. Chill.

2 Prepare a bowl of ice-cold water. Cut the turbot in half lengthways, then cut into 5mm/¼in thick slices crossways. Plunge the fish into the ice-cold water as you slice.

3 After 2 minutes or so, the fish slices will start to curl and become firm. Take out with a slotted spoon and drain on kitchen paper.

4 In a large serving bowl, mix the fish, the salad leaves and the radishes together.

5 Mix the wasabi into the dressing, add this to the salad and toss well. Serve immediately.

Nutritional information per portion: Energy 233kcal/969kJ; Protein 18.5g; Carbohydrate 1.8g, of which sugars 1.8g; Fat 16.9g, of which saturates 2.8g; Cholesterol 0mg; Calcium 77mg; Fibre 0.9g; Sodium 72mg.

Seafood salad with fruity dressing

Here, white fish is briefly seared, then served with prawns and salad tossed in an oil-free apricot and apple dressing. The fruit flavours make a delicate accompaniment to the fish.

SERVES 4

1 baby onion, sliced lengthways
lemon juice
400g/14oz very fresh sea bream or sea
    bass, filleted
30ml/2 tbsp sake
4 large king prawns (jumbo shrimp),
    heads and shells removed
about 400g/14oz mixed salad leaves

FOR THE FRUITY DRESSING

2 ripe apricots, skinned and stoned
    (pitted)
1/4 apple, peeled and cored
60ml/4 tbsp second dashi stock or the
    same amount of water and 5ml/1 tsp
    dashi-no-moto
10ml/2 tsp shoyu
salt and ground white pepper

1 Soak the onion in ice-cold water for 30 minutes. Drain. Bring a pan half-full of water to the boil. Add a dash of lemon juice and plunge the fish into it. Remove the fish after 30 seconds and cool under cold running water. Cut into 8mm/1/3in thick slices crossways.

2 Bring the sake to the boil, then add the king prawns. Cook for 1 minute, or until they turn pink.

3 Cool the prawns under cold running water and cut into 1cm/1/2in thick slices crossways.

4 Slice an apricot thinly and set aside. Purée the remaining dressing ingredients. Chill. Lay out some salad leaves on plates. Mix the fish, prawn, apricot and onion together, add the remaining leaves, then pour on the dressing and toss. Serve the dish immediately.

Nutritional information per portion: Energy 157kcal/662kJ; Protein 25g; Carbohydrate 5.3g, of which sugars 4.9g; Fat 3.2g, of which saturates 0.5g; Cholesterol 129mg; Calcium 186mg; Fibre 1.6g; Sodium 299mg.

Teppan yaki

Many Japanese homes have a portable gas cooker, a table griddle, or a table equipped with a recessed cooking surface. This is because the Japanese love cooking as they eat.

SERVES 4

275g/10oz monkfish tail

4 large scallops, cleaned and corals
　separated

250g/9oz squid body, cleaned and skinned

12 raw king or tiger prawns (jumbo
　shrimp), shells and heads removed,
　tails intact

115g/4oz/1/2 cup beansprouts, washed

1 red (bell) pepper, seeded and cut into
　2.5cm/1in wide strips

8 fresh shiitake mushrooms, stalks
　removed

1 red onion, cut into 5mm/1/4in thick
　rounds

1 courgette (zucchini), cut into 1cm/1/2in
　thick rounds

3 garlic cloves, thinly sliced lengthways

vegetable oil, for frying

**SAUCE A, RADISH AND
CHILLI SAUCE**

8 radishes, finely grated

1 dried chilli, seeded and crushed

15ml/1 tbsp toasted sesame oil

1/2 onion, finely chopped

90ml/6 tbsp shoyu

30ml/2 tbsp caster (superfine) sugar

45ml/3 tbsp toasted sesame seeds

30ml/2 tbsp unsweetened orange juice

**SAUCE B, WASABI
MAYONNAISE**

105ml/7 tbsp mayonnaise

15ml/1 tbsp wasabi paste from a tube

5ml/1 tsp shoyu

1 Sauce A: Mix the radish, its juice and the chilli in a bowl. Heat the sesame oil in a frying pan and fry the onion until soft. Pour in the shoyu and add the sugar and sesame seeds, removing the pan from the heat just as it starts to boil. Tip into the bowl and add the orange juice. Stir and cool.

2 Sauce B: Mix the mayonnaise, wasabi and shoyu together in a bowl and set aside.

3 Cut the monkfish into large, bitesize, 5mm/1/4in thick slices. Cut the scallops in half horizontally. Make shallow criss-cross slits in the skinned side of the squid. Slice into 2.5 x 4cm/1 x 11/2in pieces.

4 Put the seafood on half a platter, and arrange the vegetables (apart from the garlic) on the other half. Put sauce A in a small dish. Put the wasabi mayonnaise in a bowl.

5 Heat the griddle and oil it. Fry the garlic until crisp then transfer to a dish and mix with sauces. Fry the ingredients as you eat, dipping into the sauce or serving with mayonnaise. Oil the griddle from time to time.

Nutritional information per portion: Energy 307kcal/1273kJ; Protein 17.4g; Carbohydrate 4.2g, of which sugars 4g; Fat 23.7g, of which saturates 3.6g; Cholesterol 83mg; Calcium 91mg; Fibre 0.2g; Sodium 961mg.

Fish cakes and vegetables

Oden is a satisfying dish to make as you can buy assorted ready-made fish balls and fish cakes from Asian food stores. You will also need a large clay pot or casserole and a portable stove.

SERVES 4

30 x 7.5cm/12 x 3in dashi-konbu

675g/1¹/₂lb daikon, peeled and cut into
   4cm/1¹/₂in lengths

12–20 ready-made fish balls and cakes

1 konnyaku

1 atsu-age

8 small shiitake mushrooms, stalks
   removed

4 medium potatoes, unpeeled, soaked in a
   bowl of water

4 hard-boiled (hard-cooked) eggs, unshelled

285g/10¹/₄oz packet tofu block, cut into
   8 cubes

English (hot) mustard, to serve

FOR THE SOUP STOCK

1.5 litres/2¹/₂ pints/6¹/₄ cups second
   dashi stock, or the same amount of
   water and 10ml/2 tsp dashi-no-moto

75ml/5 tbsp sake

15ml/1 tbsp salt

40ml/8 tsp shoyu

1 Wrap the dashi-konbu in a wet dish towel for 5 minutes, or until soft enough to bend easily by hand without breaking. Snip it in half crossways, then cut each into four ribbons lengthways. Tie the centre of each "ribbon".

2 Slightly shave the edges of each of the daikon cylinders. Place all the fish balls and cakes, konnyaku and atsu-age in a large pan. Add enough hot water to cover, then drain.

3 Cut the konnyaku in quarters, then cut each quarter in half diagonally to make eight triangles. Cut large fish cakes in half. Put two shiitake mushrooms on to each of four bamboo skewers.

4 Mix all the ingredients for the soup stock, but only fill the pot or casserole by two-thirds. Add the daikon and potatoes and bring to the boil. Add the hard-boiled eggs. Reduce the heat to low and simmer for an hour, uncovered, skimming occasionally.

5 Increase the heat to medium and add the other ingredients. Cook, covered, for 30 minutes, then bring to the table cooker and keep warm on the lowest heat. Serve with mustard. Top up the pot with stock when it has reduced to half.

Nutritional information per portion: Energy 370kcal/1555kJ; Protein 37.1g; Carbohydrate 28.8g, of which sugars 5.8g; Fat 10.4g, of which saturates 2.4g; Cholesterol 236mg; Calcium 327mg; Fibre 3.1g; Sodium 1926mg.

Simmered squid and daikon

Ika To Daikon Ni *is a classic dish, the secret of which used to be handed down from mother to daughter. Nowadays, you are more likely to taste the real thing at restaurants.*

SERVES 4

450g/1lb squid, cleaned, body and
   tentacles separated
about 1kg/2¼lb daikon, peeled
900ml/1½ pints/3¾ cups second dashi
   stock or the same amount of water
   and 5ml/1 tsp dashi-no-moto
60ml/4 tbsp shoyu
45ml/3 tbsp sake
15ml/1 tbsp caster (superfine) sugar
30ml/2 tbsp mirin
grated rind of ½ yuzu or lime, to garnish

1 Separate the two triangular flaps from the squid body. Cut the body into 1cm/½in thick rings. Cut the triangular flaps into 1cm/½in strips. Finally, chop the tentacles into 4cm/1½in lengths.

2 Cut the daikon into 3cm/1¼in thick rounds and shave the edges of the sections with a sharp knife. Plunge the slices into cold water. Drain just before cooking.

3 Put the daikon and squid in a pan and pour on the stock. Bring to the boil, and cook for 5 minutes, skimming. Reduce the heat and add the shoyu, sake, sugar and mirin.

4 Cover with a circle of baking parchment and simmer for 45 minutes. Shake the pan occasionally. The liquid will reduce by almost a half. Leave for 5 minutes and serve hot with yuzu or lime rind.

Nutritional information per portion: Energy 185kcal/780kJ; Protein 19.6g; Carbohydrate 19.3g, of which sugars 17.8g; Fat 2.4g, of which saturates 0.7g; Cholesterol 253mg; Calcium 72mg; Fibre 2.3g; Sodium 1221mg.

Salmon teriyaki

Saké Teriyaki is a well-known Japanese dish, which uses a sweet and shiny sauce for marinating as well as for glazing the ingredients.

SERVES 4

4 small salmon fillets with skin on, each
   weighing about 150g/5oz
50g/2oz/¼ cup beansprouts, washed
50g/2oz mangetouts (snow peas), ends
   trimmed
20g/¾oz carrot, cut into thin strips
salt

FOR THE *TERIYAKI* SAUCE

45ml/3 tbsp shoyu
45ml/3 tbsp sake
45ml/3 tbsp mirin
15ml/1 tbsp plus 10ml/2 tsp caster
   (superfine) sugar

1 Mix all the ingredients for the sauce, except for the 10ml/2 tsp sugar, in a pan. Heat to dissolve the sugar. Remove and cool for an hour. Place the fish in a dish and pour over the sauce. Leave for 30 minutes.

2 Boil the vegetables in salted water. First add the beansprouts, then after 1 minute add the mangetouts. Leave for 1 minute, then add the carrot strips. Drain and keep warm.

3 Preheat the grill (broiler) to medium. Take the salmon out of the sauce and pat dry. Reserve the sauce. Cook the salmon for 6 minutes, turning once, until golden on both sides.

4 Pour the sauce into the pan. Add the remaining sugar and heat until dissolved. Brush the salmon with the sauce, then grill until the surface of the fish bubbles. Turn over and repeat on the other side of the salmon.

5 Serve the vegetables with the salmon. Spoon over the rest of the sauce.

Nutritional information per portion: Energy 337kcal/1408kJ; Protein 31.6g; Carbohydrate 13g, of which sugars 12.5g; Fat 16.6g, of which saturates 2.9g; Cholesterol 75mg; Calcium 49mg; Fibre 0.6g; Sodium 872mg.

Meat and poultry

Most meat recipes in Japanese cooking use meat and poultry as a rich flavouring ingredient for vegetables and rice. Even in sukiyaki, the quintessential Japanese classic, there are plenty of accompanying vegetables. Sauces and stocks are also used to enhance the flavour of the dish.

Grilled chicken balls cooked on bamboo skewers

These tasty chicken balls, called tsukune, are popular in yakitori bars and also are a favourite with children, because they can be eaten directly from the skewer.

SERVES 4

300g/11oz skinless chicken, minced (ground)
2 eggs
2.5ml/½ tsp salt
10ml/2 tsp plain (all-purpose) flour
10ml/2 tsp cornflour (cornstarch)
90ml/6 tbsp dried breadcrumbs
2.5cm/1in piece fresh root ginger, grated

FOR THE "*TARE*" *YAKITORI* SAUCE
60ml/4 tbsp sake
75ml/5 tbsp shoyu
15ml/1 tbsp mirin
15ml/1 tbsp caster (superfine) sugar
2.5ml/½ tsp cornflour (cornstarch) blended
    with 5ml/1 tsp water
shichimi togarashi or sansho, to garnish
    (optional)

1 Soak eight bamboo skewers overnight in water. Put all the ingredients for the chicken balls, except the ginger, in a food processor and blend well. Wet your hands and shape about a tablespoonful of the mixture into a small ball. Make a further 30–32 balls in the same way.

2 Squeeze the juice from the grated ginger into a bowl. Discard the pulp. Add the ginger juice to a pan of boiling water. Add the chicken balls, and boil for 7 minutes, or until the meat is brown and the balls float to the surface. Scoop out using a slotted spoon and drain on a plate covered with kitchen paper.

3 In a small pan, mix all the ingredients for the sauce, except for the cornflour liquid. Bring to the boil, then reduce the heat and simmer for 10 minutes, or until the sauce has slightly reduced. Add the cornflour liquid and stir until the sauce is thick. Transfer to a bowl.

4 Thread 3–4 balls on to each skewer. Cook under a medium grill (broiler). Turn them frequently for a few minutes, or until the balls start to brown. Brush with sauce and return to the heat. Repeat the process twice. Serve, sprinkled with shichimi togarashi or sansho, if you like.

Nutritional information per portion: Energy 332kcal/1397kJ; Protein 30.3g; Carbohydrate 29g, of which sugars 7.4g; Fat 9.7g, of which saturates 2.6g; Cholesterol 339mg; Calcium 84mg; Fibre 0.6g; Sodium 325mg.

Pot-cooked duck and green vegetables

Prepare the ingredients for this dish, **Kamo Nabe,** *beforehand, so that the cooking can be done at the table. Use a heavy pan or flameproof casserole with a portable stove.*

SERVES 4

4 duck breast fillets, about 800g/1¾lb
　　total weight
8 large shiitake mushrooms, stalks
　　removed, a cross cut into each cap
2 leeks, trimmed and cut diagonally into
　　6cm/2½in lengths
½ hakusai, stalk part removed and cut
　　into 5cm/2in squares
500g/1¼lb shungiku or mizuna, root part
　　removed, cut in half crossways

FOR THE STOCK
raw bones from 1 chicken, washed
1 egg shell
200g/7oz/scant 1 cup short grain rice,
　　washed and drained

120ml/4fl oz/½ cup sake
about 10ml/2 tsp coarse sea salt

FOR THE SAUCE
75ml/5 tbsp shoyu
30ml/2 tbsp sake
juice of 1 lime
8 white peppercorns, roughly crushed

FOR THE SOUP
130g/4½oz Chinese egg noodles, cooked
　　and loosened
1 egg, beaten
1 bunch of chives, chopped
freshly ground white pepper

1 To make the stock, put the bones into a pan three-quarters full of water. Bring to the boil and drain when it reaches boiling point. Wash the pan and bones, then return to the pan with the same amount of water. Add the egg shell and bring to the boil. Simmer for 1 hour, skimming. Remove the bones and shell. Add the rice, sake and salt and simmer for 30 minutes. Set aside.

2 Heat a frying pan until just smoking. Remove from the heat and add the duck, skin side down. Sear until crisp. Turn over and sear the other side for 1 minute. Cool.

3 Wipe the duck fat with kitchen paper and cut the breast and skin into 5mm/¼in thick slices. Arrange on a plate with the vegetables.

4 Heat through the ingredients for the sauce and transfer to a bowl.

5 Bring the soup stock to the boil, then reduce to medium-low. Add half the shiitake and leeks. Wait for 5 minutes and put in half the stalk part of the hakusai. Add half the duck and cook for 1–2 minutes for rare or 5–8 minutes for well-done.

6 Each person prepares some duck and vegetables in a serving bowl and drizzles over a little sauce. Add the hakusai leaves, shungiku and mizuna to the stock as you eat, adjusting the heat as you go. When the stock is less than a quarter of the pot's volume, top up with 3 parts water to 1 part sake.

7 When the duck has been eaten, bring the reduced stock to the boil. Skim the oil from the surface, and reduce the heat to medium. Add the noodles, cook for 1–2 minutes and check the seasoning. Add more salt if required. Pour in the beaten egg and swirl in the stock. Cover, turn off the heat, then leave to stand for 1 minute. Decorate with the chopped chives and serve with ground pepper.

Nutritional information per portion: Energy 626kcal/2633kJ; Protein 52.3g; Carbohydrate 69.4g, of which sugars 6g; Fat 18.6g, of which saturates 4g; Cholesterol 277mg; Calcium 110mg; Fibre 4.3g; Sodium 1640mg.

Cubed chicken and vegetables

A popular Japanese cooking style simmers vegetables of different textures with a small amount of meat together in dashi stock. This chicken version is known as Iridori.

SERVES 4

2 chicken thighs, about 200g/7oz, boned, with skin remaining
1 large carrot, trimmed
1 konnyaku
300g/11oz satoimo or small potatoes
500g/1¼lb canned take-no-ko, drained
30ml/2 tbsp vegetable oil
300ml/½ pint/1¼ cups water and 7.5ml/1½ tsp dashi-no-moto (stock granules)
salt

FOR THE SIMMERING SEASONINGS
75ml/5 tbsp shoyu
30ml/2 tbsp sake
30ml/2 tbsp caster (superfine) sugar
30ml/2 tbsp mirin

1 Cut the chicken into bitesize pieces. Chop the carrot into 2cm/¾in triangular chunks.

2 Boil the konnyaku for 1 minute and drain. Cool, then slice it crossways into 5mm/¼in thick rectangular strips. Cut a 4cm/1½in slit down the centre of a strip without cutting the ends. Push the top of the strip through the slit to make a tie. Repeat with all the konnyaku.

3 Peel and halve the satoimo. Put the pieces in a colander and sprinkle with salt. Rub well and wash. Drain. If using, peel and halve the potatoes.

4 Halve the take-no-ko, then cut into the same shape as the carrot.

5 Heat the oil and stir-fry the chicken until the meat turns white. Add the carrot, konnyaku, satoimo and take-no-ko. Stir each time you add a new ingredient.

6 Add the dashi and bring to the boil. Cook for 3 minutes then reduce to medium-low. Add the seasonings, cover and simmer for 15 minutes until most of the liquid has evaporated. When the satoimo is soft, transfer the chicken and vegetables to a large bowl and serve.

Nutritional information per portion: Energy 302kcal/1266kJ; Protein 20g; Carbohydrate 27.8g, of which sugars 16g; Fat 12.1g, of which saturates 1.7g; Cholesterol 39mg; Calcium 659mg; Fibre 1.2g; Sodium 1388mg.

Sumo wrestler's hotpot

*This filling hot-pot, called **Chanko Nabe**, is probably responsible for the vast size of Sumo wrestlers, as it is their first meal of the day after 4–6 hours of morning exercise. You need a Japanese clay pot or heavy pan and a portable table stove or a plate warmer.*

SERVES 4–6

2 abura-age

1 bunch of shungiku or pak choi (bok choy), 200g/7oz, root part trimmed

1 large leek, trimmed

1 daikon, thickly peeled

1/2 hakusai

1 dashi-konbu, 4 x 10cm/1^{1}/$_{2}$ x 4in

350g/12oz chicken, boned and cut into large bitesize pieces

12 shiitake mushrooms, stalks removed, a cross cut into each cap

285g/10^{1}/$_{4}$oz packet tofu block, drained and cut into 8 cubes

FOR THE FISH BALLS

6 sardines, about 350g/12oz, cleaned and filleted

2.5cm/1in fresh root ginger, chopped

1 large (US extra large) egg

25ml/1^{1}/$_{2}$ tbsp miso (any except hatcho or aka)

20 chives, roughly chopped

30ml/2 tbsp plain (all-purpose) flour

FOR THE SOUP STOCK

550ml/18fl oz/2^{1}/$_{2}$ cups sake

550ml/18fl oz/2^{1}/$_{2}$ cups water

60ml/4 tbsp shoyu

FOR THE CITRUS PEPPER (OPTIONAL)

grated rind of 1 lime

10–12 white peppercorns

1 Make the fish balls by chopping all the ingredients. Transfer to a container, cover and set aside.

2 Blanch the abura-age for 30 seconds. Drain under running water and squeeze out the water. Cut each abura-age in half lengthways, then quarter crossways to make eight rectangles. Cut each rectangle in half diagonally to make two triangles, to give 32 triangles.

3 Cut the shungiku into 6cm/2^{1}/$_{2}$in lengths. Cut the leek diagonally in 2.5cm/1in thick oval shapes. Cut the daikon into 5mm/^{1}/$_{4}$in rounds. Cut the hakusai leaves into strips crossways, keeping the leaves and stalks separate. Grind the citrus pepper ingredients and set aside.

4 Lay the dashi-konbu on the base of the pan. Pour in the ingredients for the soup stock to fill half the pan, and bring to the boil on a high heat.

5 To cook the fish balls, reduce the heat to medium. Scoop up the fish-ball paste with a spoon and shape roughly like a rugby ball. Drop into the boiling stock. Repeat until all the paste is used. Skim frequently. Cook for 3 minutes.

6 Add the chicken, daikon, the stalks of the hakusai, the shiitake and leek, then the tofu and abura-age. Simmer for 12 minutes, or until the chicken is cooked. Add the soft parts of the hakusai and the shungiku and wait for 3 minutes. Remove from the heat.

7 Put the pan on the portable stove on the table, set at the lowest heat, or on a plate warmer. Serve small amounts of the ingredients in bowls. Guests help themselves from the pot. Sprinkle on citrus pepper, if you like.

COOK'S TIP
At the end of the meal there is a tasty, rich soup left in the pot. Add 200g/7oz cooked udon noodles into the remaining soup and bring to the boil again. After 2 minutes, serve the noodles in bowls with plenty of soup and chopped chives on top.

Nutritional information per portion: Energy 311kcal/1301kJ; Protein 38.4g; Carbohydrate 5.4g, of which sugars 4.2g; Fat 15.3g, of which saturates 1.4g; Cholesterol 73mg; Calcium 1099mg; Fibre 3g; Sodium 853mg.

Grilled skewered chicken

The Japanese always accompany alcoholic drinks with nibbles, which are generally called tsumami. Grilled skewered chicken dipped in yakitori *sauce is one of the most popular.*

SERVES 4

8 chicken thighs with skin, boned and cut into 2.5cm/1in cubes

8 large, thick spring onions (scallions), trimmed and cut into 2.5cm/1in sticks

FOR THE *YAKITORI* SAUCE
60ml/4 tbsp sake
75ml/5 tbsp shoyu
15ml/1 tbsp mirin
15ml/1 tbsp caster (superfine) sugar

TO SERVE
shichimi togarashi, sansho or lemon wedges

1 First, make the sauce. Mix all the ingredients together in a pan. Bring to the boil, then reduce the heat and simmer for 10 minutes, or until the sauce has thickened.

2 Preheat the grill (broiler) to high. Oil the wire rack and arrange the chicken cubes on it. Grill both sides of the chicken until the juices drip, then dip in the sauce and return to the rack. Grill for 30 seconds on each side, repeating the dipping process twice more. Keep warm.

3 Gently grill the spring onions until soft and slightly brown. Do not dip.

4 Thread about four pieces of the grilled chicken and three grilled spring onion pieces on to each of eight bamboo skewers. Make sure the chicken and spring onions are are evenly spaced on the skewers.

5 Arrange the skewers on a large serving platter and serve sprinkled with shichimi togarashi or sansho, or accompanied by lemon wedges.

Nutritional information per portion: Energy 165kcal/695kJ; Protein 22g; Carbohydrate 9g, of which sugars 8.8g; Fat 2.9g, of which saturates 0.8g; Cholesterol 105mg; Calcium 24mg; Fibre 0.4g; Sodium 1429mg.

Simmered beef slices and vegetables

This dish, Niku Jyaga, *is a typical home-cooked meal and is one of the traditional dishes referred to as "mother's speciality". It is easy to cook and you can use inexpensive cuts of beef.*

SERVES 4

250g/9oz beef fillet (or any cut), very thinly sliced
1 large onion
15ml/1 tbsp vegetable oil
450g/1lb small potatoes, halved then soaked in water
1 carrot, cut into 5mm/¼in rounds
45ml/3 tbsp frozen peas, defrosted and blanched for 1 minute

FOR THE SEASONINGS
30ml/2 tbsp caster (superfine) sugar
75ml/5 tbsp shoyu
15ml/1 tbsp mirin
15ml/1 tbsp sake

1 Cut the thinly sliced beef slices into 2cm/¾in wide strips, and slice the onion lengthways into 5mm/¼in pieces.

2 Heat the vegetable oil in a pan and lightly fry the beef and onion slices. When the colour of the meat changes, drain the potatoes and add to the pan.

3 Once the potatoes are coated with the oil in the pan, add the carrot. Pour in just enough water to cover, then bring to the boil, skimming a few times.

4 Boil vigorously for 2 minutes, then move the potatoes to the bottom of the pan and gather all the other ingredients to sit on top of them.

5 Reduce the heat to medium-low. Add the seasonings. Simmer for 20 minutes, partially covered, or until most of the liquid has evaporated.

6 Check if the potatoes are cooked. Add the peas and cook to heat through, then remove the pan from the heat. Serve the beef and vegetables immediately in four small serving bowls.

Nutritional information per portion: Energy 276kcal/1160kJ; Protein 17.8g; Carbohydrate 31.5g, of which sugars 13.2g; Fat 9.2g, of which saturates 2.9g; Cholesterol 36mg; Calcium 28mg; Fibre 2.3g; Sodium 1394mg.

Sliced seared beef

*Japanese chefs use a cooking technique called **tataki** to cook rare steak. They normally use a coal fire and sear a chunk of beef on long skewers, then plunge it into cold water to stop it cooking further. Use a wire mesh grill over the heat source to cook this way.*

SERVES 4

500g/1¼lb chunk of beef thigh (a long, thin chunk looks better than a thick, round chunk)
generous pinch of salt
10ml/2 tsp vegetable oil

FOR THE MARINADE
200ml/7fl oz/scant 1 cup rice vinegar
70ml/4½ tbsp sake
135ml/4½fl oz/scant ⅔ cup shoyu

15ml/1 tbsp caster (superfine) sugar
1 garlic clove, thinly sliced
1 small onion, thinly sliced
sansho

FOR THE GARNISH
6 shiso leaves and shiso flowers (if available)
about 15cm/6in Japanese or ordinary salad cucumber
½ lemon, thinly sliced
1 garlic clove, finely grated (optional)

1 Mix the marinade ingredients in a small pan and warm through until the sugar has dissolved. Remove from the heat and leave to cool. Sprinkle the beef with the salt and rub into the meat. Leave for 2–3 minutes, then rub the oil in evenly. Fill a large bowl with water. Heat a griddle. Sear the beef, turning until a depth of 5mm/¼in of the flesh is cooked. Immediately plunge the meat into the water for a few seconds. Wipe the meat and immerse fully in the marinade for 1 day.

2 Next day, slice the shiso leaves into thin strips. Slice the cucumber diagonally into oval shapes, then cut each oval into matchsticks. Remove the meat from the marinade. Strain the remaining marinade, reserving both the liquid and the marinated onion and garlic. Cut the beef into thin slices.

3 Heap the cucumber on a serving plate and put the onion and garlic on top. Arrange the beef leaning alongside. Or, if the slices are large enough, you could roll them. Fluff the shiso strips and put on top of the beef. Decorate with shiso flowers, if using.

4 To eat, take a few beef slices. Roll a slice with your choice of garnish, then dip it into the marinade. Add a little grated garlic, if you like.

Nutritional information per portion: Energy 258kcal/1079kJ; Protein 28.7g; Carbohydrate 9.8g, of which sugars 9.8g; Fat 11.7g, of which saturates 4.8g; Cholesterol 73mg; Calcium 20mg; Fibre 0.3g; Sodium 82mg.

Sukiyaki

You will need a sukiyaki *pan or a shallow cast-iron pan, and a portable table stove to cook this traditional dish of beef and vegetables.*

SERVES 4

600g/1lb 6oz well-marbled beef sirloin, without bone, sliced thinly
15ml/1 tbsp sake
1 packet shirataki noodles, about 200g/7oz, drained
10 spring onions (scallions), trimmed and quartered diagonally lengthways
2 large onions, cut into 8 slices lengthways
450g/1lb enokitake mushrooms, trimmed
12 shiitake mushrooms, stalks removed
300g/11oz shungiku, cut in half lengthways, or watercress
250–275g/9–10oz tofu, drained and cut into 8–12 large bitesize cubes
4–8 very fresh eggs, at room temperature
about 20g/³⁄₄oz beef fat

FOR THE *WARI-SHITA* SAUCE
75ml/5 tbsp second dashi stock, or the same amount of water and 5ml/1 tsp dashi-no-moto
75ml/5 tbsp shoyu
120ml/4fl oz/¹⁄₂ cup mirin
15ml/1 tbsp sake
15ml/1 tbsp caster (superfine) sugar

1 Arrange the beef on a large plate. Sprinkle with the sake. Par-boil the shirataki in rapidly boiling water for 2 minutes, then drain. Wash and cut into 5cm/2in lengths. Drain well. Heat all the ingredients for the *wari-shita* sauce over medium heat until the sugar has dissolved. Pour the sauce into a bowl.

2 On a tray, arrange the vegetables, shirataki and tofu. Break one egg into each of four small serving bowls. Start cooking when the guests are seated. Heat the pan on a table cooker until very hot, reduce the heat to medium, and add some beef fat. When it has melted, add the spring onions and onion slices. Increase the heat and stir-fry for 2 minutes, or until the onions are soft. The guests should now start to beat the egg in their bowls.

3 Add a quarter of the *wari-shita* sauce to the pan. When it starts to bubble, add a quarter of the vegetables, tofu and shirataki. Add four slices of beef to the pan. As they change colour, remove them immediately from the pan and dip into the egg. Cook the vegetables and other ingredients in the same way. Add more sauce when it is reduced in the pan.

Nutritional information per portion: Energy 868kcal/3633kJ; Protein 71.5g; Carbohydrate 51.7g, of which sugars 11.1g; Fat 43.2g, of which saturates 13.1g; Cholesterol 662mg; Calcium 605mg; Fibre 6.5g; Sodium 1695mg.

Pan-fried pork

Created by a dinner lady at a Tokyo university in the 1970s, this is popular with youngsters.

SERVES 4

450g/1lb pork chops, boned and trimmed
15ml/1 tbsp vegetable oil
1 small onion, thinly sliced lengthways
50g/2oz/¼ cup beansprouts
50g/2oz mangetouts (snow peas), trimmed
salt

FOR THE MARINADE
15ml/1 tbsp shoyu
15ml/1 tbsp sake
15ml/1 tbsp mirin
4cm/1½in piece fresh root ginger,
   very finely grated, plus juice

1 Freeze the pork for 2 hours. Cut into 3mm/⅛in slices, then into 4cm/1½in wide strips.

2 Mix all the marinade ingredients together. Add the pork and marinate for 15 minutes.

3 Heat the oil in a frying pan. Add the onion and fry for 3 minutes. Take half the pork out from the marinade and add to the pan. Transfer the meat to a plate when its colour changes. Repeat with the rest of the meat. Reserve the marinade. Add the onions to the plate.

4 Pour the marinade into the pan and simmer until it has reduced by one-third. Add the beansprouts and mangetouts, then the pork and increase the heat to medium-high for 2 minutes. Serve.

Nutritional information per portion: Energy 176kcal/738kJ; Protein 25.2g; Carbohydrate 2.4g, of which sugars 1.7g; Fat 7.4g, of which saturates 1.9g; Cholesterol 71mg; Calcium 20mg; Fibre 0.7g; Sodium 258mg.

Deep-fried pork fillet

Known as Ton-katsu, *some Japanese restaurants serve just this one dish.*

SERVES 4

4 pork loin chops or cutlets, boned
plain (all-purpose) flour, to dust
vegetable oil, for deep-frying
2 eggs, beaten
50g/2oz/1 cup dried white breadcrumbs
1 white cabbage, finely sliced
salt and ready-ground mixed pepper
prepared English (hot) mustard, to serve
Japanese pickles, to serve

FOR THE *TON-KATSU* SAUCE
60ml/4 tbsp Worcestershire sauce
30ml/2 tbsp good-quality tomato ketchup
5ml/1 tsp shoyu

1 Make a few cuts horizontally across the fat of the meat. Rub seasoning into the meat and dust with flour, shaking off any excess. Heat the oil in a deep-fryer or pan to 180°C/350°F.

2 Dip the meat in the eggs, then coat with breadcrumbs. Deep-fry two pieces at a time for 8–10 minutes until golden brown. Drain on kitchen paper.

3 Put the cabbage on four plates. Cut the pork crossways into 2cm/¾in thick strips and place on the cabbage.

4 For the *ton-katsu* sauce, mix the Worcestershire sauce, ketchup and shoyu in a jug (pitcher). Serve the pork immediately, with the sauce, mustard and pickles.

Nutritional information per portion: Energy 385kcal/1607kJ; Protein 30.9g; Carbohydrate 19.3g, of which sugars 9.6g; Fat 21g, of which saturates 4.2g; Cholesterol 253mg; Calcium 131mg; Fibre 2.5g; Sodium 633mg.

Roasted and marinated pork

Yuan, a sauce made from sake, shoyu, mirin and citrus fruit, is often used to marinate ingredients either before or after cooking. If possible, leave the meat to marinate overnight.

SERVES 4

600g/1lb 6oz pork fillet (tenderloin)
1 garlic clove, crushed
generous pinch of salt
4 spring onions (scallions), trimmed,
    white part only
10g/¼oz dried wakame, soaked in water
    for 20 minutes and drained
10cm/4in celery stick, trimmed and cut in
    half crossways
1 carton mustard and cress

FOR THE *YUAN* SAUCE

105ml/7 tbsp shoyu
45ml/3 tbsp sake
60ml/4 tbsp mirin
1 lime, sliced into thin rings

1 Preheat the oven to 200°C/400°F/Gas 6. Rub the pork with the garlic and salt. Leave for 15 minutes.

2 Roast the pork for 20 minutes, then turn it over and reduce the temperature to 180°C/350°F/Gas 4. Cook for a further 20 minutes.

3 Mix the sauce ingredients. Transfer the pork to the sauce and marinate for 2 hours, or overnight. Finely shred the spring onions. Soak in ice-cold water. When the shreds curl up, drain and gather them into a loose ball.

4 Cut the drained wakame into 2.5cm/1in squares or narrow strips. Slice the celery very thinly lengthways. Soak it in a bowl of cold water, then drain and gather it together in a loose ball as before.

5 Remove the pork from the marinade and wipe with kitchen paper. Slice the pork very thinly.

6 Strain the marinade into a small jug (pitcher) or bowl. Arrange the sliced pork on a large serving platter with all the vegetables around it and serve cold with the *yuan* sauce.

Nutritional information per portion: Energy 241kcal/1015kJ; Protein 33.4g; Carbohydrate 10.6g, of which sugars 10.3g; Fat 6.2g, of which saturates 2.1g; Cholesterol 95mg; Calcium 33mg; Fibre 0.4g; Sodium 1983mg.

Desserts and baking

Glutinous rice, azuki beans, squash, sweet

potatoes and sugar are the most commonly

used ingredients in Japanese desserts;

dairy foods are rarely used. It is not

customary in Japan to have a dessert after

a meal, so the dishes here are eaten as

an accompaniment to Japanese tea.

Green tea ice cream

In the past, the Japanese did not follow a meal with dessert, apart from some fruit. This custom is changing and many Japanese restaurants offer light desserts such as sorbet or ice cream.

SERVES 4

500ml/17fl oz carton good-quality vanilla ice cream
15ml/1 tbsp matcha
15ml/1 tbsp lukewarm water from the kettle

1 Soften the ice cream in the refrigerator for 20–30 minutes.

2 Mix the matcha powder and lukewarm water to a smooth paste.

3 Put half the ice cream into a mixing bowl. Add the matcha liquid and mix with a rubber spatula.

4 Add the rest of the ice cream. You can stop mixing when the ice cream looks a marbled dark green and white, or continue mixing until the ice cream is a uniform pale green. Put the bowl into the freezer.

5 After 1 hour, the ice cream is ready. Scoop into bowls to serve.

Nutritional information per portion: Energy 269kcal/1120kJ; Protein 4.9g; Carbohydrate 21.1g, of which sugars 21g; Fat 18.9g, of which saturates 11.3g; Cholesterol 0mg; Calcium 126mg; Fibre 0g; Sodium 75mg.

Sweet pancake

In Japan, the sweet bean paste is traditionally sandwiched between two pancakes to resemble a little gong. Alternatively, the pancakes can be folded to make a half gong.

MAKES 6–8 PANCAKES

65g/2¹⁄₂oz/5 tbsp caster (superfine)
   sugar
3 large (US extra large) eggs, beaten
15ml/1 tbsp maple syrup or golden
   (light corn) syrup
185g/6¹⁄₂oz/1²⁄₃ cups plain
   (all-purpose) flour, sifted
5ml/1 tsp bicarbonate of soda
   (baking soda)
150ml/¹⁄₄ pint/²⁄₃ cup water
vegetable oil, for frying

FOR THE SWEET BEAN PASTE

250g/9oz canned azuki beans
40g/1¹⁄₂oz/3 tbsp caster sugar
pinch of salt

1 To make the bean paste, put the beans and their liquid into a pan, then heat over a medium heat. Add the sugar gradually and stir. Cook until the liquid has almost evaporated and the beans are mushy. Add the salt, remove from the heat, stir for 1 minute, then cool.

2 Mix the sugar, eggs and syrup until the sugar has dissolved, then add the flour to make a smooth batter. Cover. Leave for 20 minutes.

3 Mix together the bicarbonate of soda and water in a cup and mix into the batter.

4 Heat a little oil in a frying pan until hot. Remove from the heat and wipe with kitchen paper. Return to a medium heat and ladle some batter into the centre. Make a pancake about 13cm/5in in diameter and 5mm/¹⁄₄in thick. Cook for 2–3 minutes on each side until golden brown. Make 11–15 pancakes.

5 Take one pancake and spread about 30ml/2 tbsp of the bean paste in the middle leaving about 2.5cm/1in around the edge. Cover with another pancake. Repeat until all the pancakes are used. Serve warm or cold.

Nutritional information per portion: Energy 222kcal/941kJ; Protein 7.2g; Carbohydrate 38.9g, of which sugars 15.8g; Fat 5.3g, of which saturates 1g; Cholesterol 71mg; Calcium 106mg; Fibre 1.8g; Sodium 117mg.

Sweet azuki bean paste jelly

In this summery dessert, a dark red kanten and sweet bean cube is captured in a clear kanten jelly. It resembles a small stone trapped in a block of mountain ice.

SERVES 12

200g/7oz can azuki beans, drained
40g/1^1/$_2$oz/3 tbsp caster (superfine)
   sugar

FOR THE KANTEN JELLY
2 x 5g/^{1}/$_8$oz sachets powdered kanten
100g/3^3/$_4$oz/^{1}/$_2$ cup caster sugar
rind of ^{1}/$_4$ orange in one piece

1 Tip the beans into a pan over a medium heat. When steam begins to rise, reduce the heat to low. Add the sugar one-third at a time, stirring until the sugar has dissolved and the moisture evaporated. Remove from the heat.

2 Pour 450ml/^{3}/$_4$ pint/scant 2 cups water into a pan, and mix with one kanten sachet. Stir until dissolved, then add 40g/1^1/$_2$oz of the sugar and the orange rind. Bring to the boil and cook for 2 minutes, stirring until the sugar has dissolved. Remove from the heat and discard the orange rind.

3 Transfer 250ml/8fl oz/1 cup of the hot liquid into a 15 x 10cm/6 x 4in container. Leave to set.

4 Add the bean paste to the kanten liquid, and mix. Move the pan on to a wet dish towel and keep stirring for 8 minutes. Pour the bean liquid into an 18 x 7.5 x 2cm/7 x 3 x ^{3}/$_4$in container and leave for 1 hour at room temperature, then 1 hour in the refrigerator. Turn upside down on a board covered with kitchen paper. Leave for 1 minute, then cut into 12 rectangular pieces.

5 Line 12 ramekins with clear film (plastic wrap). With a fork, cut the set kanten block into 12 squares. Put one square in each ramekin, then place a bean and kanten cube on top of each.

6 Pour 450ml/^{3}/$_4$ pint/scant 2 cups water into a pan and mix with the remaining kanten sachet. Bring to the boil, add the remaining sugar, then stir until dissolved. Boil for a further 2 minutes, and remove from the heat. Place the pan on a wet dish towel to cool and stir for 5 minutes, or until the liquid starts to thicken.

7 Ladle the liquid into the ramekins. Twist the clear film at the top. Chill for at least 1 hour. Carefully remove the ramekins and clear film and serve cold.

Nutritional information per portion: Energy 65kcal/278kJ; Protein 1.5g; Carbohydrate 15.5g, of which sugars 12.4g; Fat 0.1g, of which saturates 0g; Cholesterol 0mg; Calcium 10mg; Fibre 0.6g; Sodium 2mg.

Kabocha squash cake

Yokan (cake) is a very sweet dessert often made with azuki beans, to be eaten at tea time with green tea. In this version kabocha squash is used instead of azuki and the cake is served with fruit.

SERVES 4

1 x 350g/12oz kabocha squash
30ml/2 tbsp plain (all-purpose) flour
15ml/1 tbsp cornflour (cornstarch)
10ml/2 tsp caster (superfine) sugar
1.5ml/¼ tsp salt
1.5ml/¼ tsp ground cinnamon
25ml/1½ tbsp water
2 egg yolks, beaten

TO SERVE
½ nashi, peeled, trimmed and sliced
    thinly lengthways
½ kaki, peeled, trimmed and sliced
    thinly lengthways (optional)

1 Cut off the hard part from the top and bottom of the kabocha, then cut it into three to four wedges. Scoop out the seeds. Cut into chunks. Steam the kabocha for about 15 minutes over a medium heat. Check if a chopstick can be pushed into the centre easily. Remove and leave, covered, for 5 minutes.

2 Remove the skin from the kabocha. Mash the flesh and push it through a sieve using a wooden spoon, or use a food processor. Transfer the flesh to a bowl, add the rest of the cake ingredients, and mix well.

3 Roll out the makisu sushi mat as if making a sushi roll. Wet some muslin (cheesecloth) slightly with water and lay it on the mat. Spread the kabocha mixture evenly. Hold the nearest end and roll up the makisu to the other end. Close both outer ends by rolling up or folding the muslin over. Put the rolled kabocha in the makisu back into the steamer for 5 minutes. Remove from the heat and leave to set for 5 minutes.

4 Open the makisu when the roll has cooled down. Cut the cake into 2.5cm/1in thick slices and serve cold with the nashi and kaki, if using.

Nutritional information per portion: Energy 91kcal/382kJ; Protein 2.8g; Carbohydrate 13.8g, of which sugars 4.2g; Fat 3.1g, of which saturates 0.9g; Cholesterol 101mg; Calcium 50mg; Fibre 1.1g; Sodium 7mg.

Steamed cake with sweet potatoes and shiro miso

This soft steamed cake, known as Mushi-kasutera, *is not too sweet, and can be eaten like bread. The secret is a little miso.*

SERVES 4

200g/7oz/scant 2 cups plain (all-purpose) flour
140g/4³/₄oz/scant ³/₄ cup caster (superfine) sugar
45ml/3 tbsp sweetened condensed milk
4 eggs, beaten
40g/1¹/₂oz shiro miso
150g/5oz sweet potatoes, trimmed and peeled
10ml/2 tsp cream of tartar
2.5ml/¹/₂ tsp bicarbonate of soda (baking soda)
30ml/2 tbsp melted butter

1 Sift the flour and sugar into a bowl. In another bowl, beat the condensed milk, eggs and shiro miso until smooth. Add to the flour and mix. Leave for 1 hour.

2 Cut the sweet potatoes into 2cm/³/₄in dice. Cover with water. Drain just before using. Preheat the steamer, and line with muslin (cheesecloth).

3 Mix the cream of tartar and bicarbonate of soda with 15ml/1 tbsp water. Add to the cake mixture with the melted butter and two-thirds of the diced sweet potato. Pour the cake mixture into the steamer, then push the rest of the sweet potato on to the surface of the cake.

4 Steam the cake for 30 minutes, or until risen to a dome shape. Serve warm or cold, cut into wedges.

Nutritional information per portion: Energy 512kcal/2165kJ; Protein 12.9g; Carbohydrate 90.5g, of which sugars 46.5g; Fat 13.6g, of which saturates 6.3g; Cholesterol 210mg; Calcium 162mg; Fibre 2.5g; Sodium 862mg.

Sticky rice cake wrapped in sweet azuki bean paste

This tea-time snack, Ohagi, *is an absolute favourite among all ages in Japan. It is made on occasions such as birthdays and festivals.*

MAKES 12

150g/5oz glutinous rice
50g/2oz Japanese short grain rice
410g/14¹/₄oz can azuki beans (canned in water, with sugar and salt)
90g/3¹/₂oz/6¹/₂ tbsp caster (superfine) sugar
pinch of salt
camellia petals, to decorate (optional)

1 Wash the two kinds of rice in a sieve under cold running water, then drain. Leave for 1 hour to dry. Tip the rice into a casserole, and add 200ml/7fl oz/scant 1 cup water. Cover and bring to the boil. Reduce the heat and simmer for 15 minutes. Leave for 5 minutes. Remove the lid, cover with a towel and cool.

2 Pour the azuki beans into a pan. Over a medium heat, add the sugar one-third at a time, mixing after each addition. Reduce the heat and mash the beans. Add salt and heat to remove excess liquid. Cool.

3 Wet your hands. Shape the rice into 12 small balls. Spread 30ml/2 tbsp of the bean paste 5mm/¹/₄in thick in the centre of damp muslin (cheesecloth). Put a rice ball in the middle, then wrap up in the paste with the muslin. Repeat until all the rice balls are used. Decorate with camellia petals, if using.

Nutritional information per portion: Energy 128kcal/541kJ; Protein 4.3g; Carbohydrate 27.2g, of which sugars 8.2g; Fat 0.5g, of which saturates 0.1g; Cholesterol 0mg; Calcium 14mg; Fibre 1.2g; Sodium 3mg.

The guide to Japanese cooking

This section looks at seasonal and regional

food and the development of Japanese

cuisine. There is information on all the

different ingredients used in Japanese

cooking, such as rice, noodles, tofu,

mushrooms, seaweeds and fish; a section

on ready-made sauces; and advice on

preparation and cooking techniques.

Cooking and eating

The philosophy of Japanese cooking is to serve food that has retained as much of its natural flavour as possible. It is therefore essential to choose ingredients at their best – they should be very fresh and in their season. If the food needs to be cooked at all this is done for the minimum time possible.

PREPARATION AND COOKING METHODS

The most important aspect of Japanese cooking lies in the preparation. As the food is eaten with hashi (chopsticks), it needs to be cut into bitesize pieces. Vegetables of various shapes and textures are cooked to the correct crunchy softness so that they will be appetizing as well as attractive. Fresh fish is almost always filleted and often thinly sliced to eat raw as *sashimi*. Meats are also thinly sliced most of the time or else minced (ground) meat is used.

If the food, especially vegetables, is to be cooked, it is always very lightly done to retain crispness. Cooking methods include simmering, grilling (broiling), steaming and frying; roasting is not really part of the

BELOW: *Meal time at* ryokan, *a Japanese old-style inn. Each diner's food is served on an individual legged tray.*

Japanese cuisine. Many fish and vegetable dishes involve griddling over a direct heat, but in modern houses this is not done due to the smoke produced, in which case pan-frying may be substituted. Japanese cooking also uses various pickling and marinating methods.

TYPICAL MEALS

The traditional Japanese breakfast is a substantial meal. It consists of a bowl of hot, freshly boiled rice, miso soup, thick omelette roll, pickled vegetables and grilled (broiled) small salted fish such as horse mackerel. Today, however, busy people, particularly the young, prefer Western-style ready-made foods such as bread, ham and cheese plus salad and fruits with tea or coffee.

For lunch, Japanese soba (buckwheat noodles), udon (flour noodles) and Chinese-style ramen (egg noodles) are very popular at home and in restaurants, while single-dish meals include a tonkatsu rice bowl, a *bento* (lunch) box or curry.

Dinner at home in Japan is a rather casual affair, with each member of the family having a bowl of rice and miso soup probably with an individual main dish of either fish or meat. Two or three other dishes such as simmered vegetables, marinated fish and pickles will be placed in the centre of the table for everyone to help themselves. Second servings of rice and soup are available, and fruit and green tea are always served to finish the meal.

MENU PLANNING

A formal Japanese banquet will start with hors d'oeuvres, clear soup and *sashimi* (thinly sliced raw fish) followed in turn by a grilled dish, a steamed dish, a simmered dish and finally a deep-fried dish, accompanied by salads. The meal finishes with boiled rice, miso soup and pickles. All dishes are served individually on a tray. Fresh fruit and green tea usually end the lengthy banquet. Warmed sake is drunk throughout the meal until the rice is served.

At home a simpler traditional dinner will consist of individual bowls of soup and boiled rice with at least three main dishes, each one cooked differently: for example, *sashimi*, a grilled dish and a simmered dish. They are placed in the centre of the table for all the family to serve themselves.

For dinner parties at home, a standard menu consists of a plate of hors d'oeuvres to accompany drinks (when a toast may be made) followed by a first course, the main dish and then bowls of rice and soup with some pickles. Sake or grape wine is not served after the rice has arrived. Fruit and green tea end the meal.

ABOVE: *Eating out in Tokyo's Ginza district is popular with many Japanese.*

DRINK

There have been many attempts in the West to find out which wine goes best with Japanese food, and some food and wine experts even claim Champagne best suits the cuisine. However, nothing really matches the mellow, delicate flavour of sake because it does not override the subtle nature of Japanese cuisine. Moreover, while wine may have been developed to complement the food, it was the other way round with sake.

The Japanese drink lager beer more than any other drink and often start a meal with a glass of ice-cold lager. The lager is usually followed by sake, which is drunk cold in summer and warm in winter, or by shochu (a very alcoholic rough sake). A popular way of drinking shochu is to dilute it with hot water and add an umeboshi (dried salted Japanese apricot) to it.

Shaping Japanese rice

When making individual *su-meshi* blocks don't worry if the blocks don't look very neat. To make them perfectly requires at least two years' practice in a sushi restaurant kitchen.

To shape Japanese rice, make everything wet – from your hands to the mould, if using – and keep the work surface tidy at all times. Use both hands to squeeze the rice into a densely packed shape.

Using moulds

When making moulded sushi, one option is to use small plastic moulds, which are easily available. Otherwise line an eggcup with clear film (plastic wrap), push a topping in, add a dab of wasabi paste, then fill with *su-meshi*. Seal the end with the clear film and press with your fingers. When ready, remove from the eggcup and unwrap from the clear film.

Storage

Rice tastes best when newly harvested, and then it gradually deteriorates. Although it keeps for a long time, it is best eaten as soon as possible. Transfer raw rice to an earthenware, ceramic or plastic container with a lid and keep it in an airy, cool place away from direct sunlight. Keep rice perfectly dry; if the moisture content creeps up, the rice will soon turn mouldy. In the West rice is powdered with preservatives, hence its longevity.

Mochi with cheese and nori seaweed

This quick and easy snack is a tasty introduction to mochi.

1 Slice some Cheddar cheese a little smaller than the mochi cakes and about 5mm/¼in thick.

2 Grill (broil) the mochi cakes on each side under a medium heat for 2–3 minutes, turning them frequently to prevent burning. While the grilled mochi are still hot, make a horizontal slit at the side of each one and insert a cheese slice.

3 Cut an 18–20cm/7–8in nori sheet into four to eight pieces and wrap one piece around each of the mochi cakes before serving with a little shoyu.

ABOVE: *Shiratama flour is mainly used for making wagashi (Japanese cakes) and sweet dumplings for desserts.*

ABOVE: *Mochi (rice cakes), made from mochigome rice, are traditional fare for New Year's Day.*

ABOVE: *Nuka (rice bran) is most valued for its strong flavour and is a good base for pickling vegetables.*

RICE PRODUCTS

It is no surprise that the Japanese have developed various products out of rice and that these, in turn, have found a secure place in Japanese cooking.

Shiratama

This flour is comprised mostly of starch taken from mochigome (glutinous rice), which is first soaked in water, then sieved and dried. Shiratama is mostly used to make wagashi, which are Japanese cakes, and sweet dumplings.

Mochi

The main product of mochigome (glutinous rice) is mochi (rice cakes). Mochi cakes were once made by hand. The cooked rice was pounded until smooth, then shape and dried into a block then cut into shapes and fried, grilled (broiled) or boiled. Mochi can be made at home, but excellent ready-made cakes are available.

Domyoji

Mochigome rice is finely crushed to produce this flour, which is generally used for making wagashi (Japanese traditional cakes) and sometimes for cooking, usually in steamed dishes.

Nuka

This rice bran is traditionally used for pickling vegetables. The rice bran is first lightly roasted to bring out its flavour, then mixed with brine to make a mash, which ferments and makes a unique pickling base.

BELOW: *Sticky red rice is served in fresh edible oak leaves.*

LEFT: *Usually white, these hiyamugi noodles have occasional brown and pale pink strands.*

GENERAL PREPARATION AND COOKING TIPS

Whether fresh or dried, all noodles need to be boiled, and this should be done carefully to prevent them becoming too soft. Follow the instructions on the packet. Cut a strand in the middle to check the noodles are cooked. If the noodles are to be eaten in hot soup, boil them until they are still a little hard. If they are to be eaten cold, cook thoroughly. Once boiled, wash off the outer starch under cold running water.

Japanese noodles except ramen are eaten simply, either on their own or with a few added ingredients and rarely with meat. Ramen tends to be cooked with meat-based ingredients.

HIYAMUGI

These thin, white noodles are made in the same way as udon but cut very thinly. They take about 5 minutes to cook and are eaten in hot soup or with a dipping sauce. Dried and bundled hiyamugi is available in packets at Asian supermarkets.

RAMEN

Literally meaning stretched noodle, ramen originated in China, and is made of wheat flour with added eggs and what the Japanese call *kansui*, alkali water. The chemical reaction between them makes the wheat dough smooth and stretchable to create very fine noodles. Pure, naturally formed *kansui* is now hard to obtain and is often substituted with bicarbonate of soda (baking soda). Ramen is eaten with other cooked food with or without soup. Ramen is available fresh, dried or frozen at large supermarkets and Asian stores.

CULINARY USES

All Japanese noodles can be cooked in hot dashi-based soup with a few added ingredients, or eaten cold with a dipping sauce. Somen is a useful ingredient because of its white, almost hair-like fineness and is often used in clear soups or as a garnish. Ramen is always cooked in hot meat-based soup or eaten cold.

RIGHT: *Instant ramen noodles are usually sold with a flavoured soup sachet.*

Making handmade udon

MAKES 675G/1¹/₂LB

1 Sift 225g/8oz/2 cups plain (all-purpose) flour into a mixing bowl and make a well in the centre.

2 Dissolve 15ml/1 tbsp salt in 150ml/¹/₄ pint/²/₃ cup water, then pour liquid into the well in the centre of the flour. Using a wooden spoon, gently fold in until the mixture becomes a firm dough.

3 Turn the dough out on to a floured work surface and knead until it feels smooth but is still firm. Hit the dough hard with a fist at least 100 times to remove any air pockets. Cover with a damp cloth and leave for 2 hours.

4 Roll the dough out on a lightly floured work surface to make a rectangular sheet, 3mm/¹/₈in thick. Dust the pastry sheet lightly with flour, then fold one long side of pastry into the centre.

5 Carefully turn the pastry over, dust with flour again and fold the remaining third over the top. (If you look at the end of the folded dough, it will form an S-shape.) Fold the dough in half lengthways.

6 Using a sharp knife, cut the folded dough crossways into 3mm/¹/₈in thick strips. Separate the strands with your hands. The udon noodles can be frozen at this stage.

7 Bring plenty of water to the boil in a large, deep pan. Add the udon and cook for about 25–30 minutes, adding some cold water each time it starts to boil, until the noodles are thoroughly cooked but still slightly firm.

8 Drain the udon and wash well under cold running water to remove the outer starch from the noodles.

9 When you are ready to eat the udon noodles, you can either reheat them in a soup or quickly plunge them into a pan of boiling water. Drain the noodles well and serve with a dipping sauce of your choice.

COOK'S TIP

To check if the noodles are cooked, carefully cut a strip of udon and if the core of the cut face is turning from white to grey, then it's done.

To make a dipping sauce for cold udon, mix 2.5ml/¹/₂ tsp dashi, 45ml/3 tbsp shoyu and 15ml/1 tbsp mirin or 10ml/2 tsp sugar with 120ml/4fl oz/¹/₂ cup hot or cold water. Stir well and divide the sauce into individual serving cups. Serve with cold udon and some chopped spring onion and grated ginger.

Tofu

One of the oldest processed foods of South-east Asia, tofu has become more widely appreciated in recent years due to health-conscious trends around the world. Tofu came to Japan from China in the 8th century and has been one of the most important foods ever since.

As with many other foods, the Japanese developed tofu to a more refined form, as well as producing many new by-products to suit the subtlety and delicacy of Japanese cooking. Tofu is mostly made commercially nowadays, but there are still small tofu-making businesses in many residential areas of Japan, making fresh tofu at dawn every day.

TYPES OF TOFU

Highly nutritious and low in fat and sugar, tofu is made from soya beans, which are first boiled and crushed, then the milk is separated and made into curds with the help of a coagulant. The warm curds are set in moulds for a few hours, then released into a water tank to firm and cool further. A cotton cloth is laid across the base of the moulds to retain the curds while they set and to allow excess water to drain away. Tofu made in this way often has a distinctive cloth mark on its sides and is known as regular tofu. This tofu is called momen-goshi (cotton-sieved tofu), as opposed to the more delicate, softer kinu-goshi (silk-sieved tofu – sold as silken tofu in the West), which is made with thicker milk and without draining the excess water. Both are creamy white in colour.

Japanese tofu, both fresh and in cartons, is available from Asian supermarkets in the West. There is also lightly seared tofu called yaki-dofu, which is available from Japanese shops and is mainly used in hotpot dishes. Other lesser-quality types of tofu are widely available from supermarkets.

Aroma and flavour

To the Japanese palate, little of the tofu available outside Japan has the real taste of tofu. Although some fresh tofu has a faint soya bean aroma and milky flavour, many varieties appear to be made of little more than milky water.

Culinary uses

Fresh tofu, silken tofu in particular, is best eaten as it is, cold or hot, with shoyu, chopped spring onion (scallion) and grated ginger, or in soups. The firmer cotton tofu is more suitable for cooking dishes such as *agedashi-dofu* (fried tofu in dashi sauce) and as tofu steaks. Tofu is also cooked with other vegetables, fish and meat, and used for making a white dressing for salads.

Preparation and cooking

Tofu is extremely fragile, so handle with care. Silken tofu is normally used as it is, but cotton tofu, if it is going to be fried or mashed to make a dressing, is normally pressed to squeeze out some water to make it a little firmer.

BELOW: *Clockwise from front left, soft or silken tofu, lightly seared tofu and regular, firmer tofu.*

KOYA-DOFU

Also known as kogori-dofu (frozen tofu), koya-dofu is believed to have been invented by Buddhist monks on the Koya mountain many centuries ago. It is a freeze-dried tofu, and is quite different from regular tofu in texture, colour, flavour and size.

Today, koya-dofu is often available in packets of five pieces together with a powdered soup stock in which to cook it. When purchased this way it simply requires cooking in the soup provided. This modern version is readily available.

Aroma and flavour

Koya-dofu has a much stronger soya bean aroma and richer flavour than cotton or silken tofu. The beauty of this spongy tofu is that, however long it is cooked, it does not disintegrate.

Culinary uses

Because of its spongy nature, koya-dofu absorbs flavours well, so it is used for simmering with vegetables in a rich soup.

Preparation and cooking

If the packet does not contain sachets of powdered soup, koya-dofu needs soaking in hot water for 5 minutes before cooking. However, most koya-dofu is now made so that it can be cooked immediately in the powdered soup provided in the packet.

RIGHT: *Abura-age (thin deep-fried tofu) is the most commonly used tofu in Japanese cooking and is available fresh or frozen.*

YUBA

This is the dried soya bean skin that forms on the surface of the soya bean milk during the tofu-making process. Sold in packets, it comes in various sheet forms, including flat, rolled and cut, or in thick strips, and is becoming more available from Japanese stores.

Aroma and flavour

Once cooked in soup, yuba gives out a warm soya bean aroma and has a rich, milky flavour with a crunchy texture.

Culinary uses

Yuba is used mainly in clear soups and simmered dishes. It is one of Kyoto's specialities and is often used in their version of the *kaiseki* (formal banquet).

Preparation and cooking

Soften yuba in tepid water for 5 minutes before cooking. Although it does not disintegrate, cook only very lightly.

FRIED TOFU

There are various types of fried tofu commercially produced and commonly used for home cooking in Japan. They are, like tofu, freshly made every day by neighbourhood tofu makers and sold like freshly baked bread. In the West some deep-fried tofu are also freshly made and sold refrigerated at Japanese supermarkets.

Mushrooms

The mushroom is a fungus whose developed offshoots grow in or under certain trees. In a relatively warm and wet country in which over 75 per cent of the land is covered by mountains, mushrooms grow in abundance and are used in everyday cooking.

Apart from the most popular ones, introduced below, there are the Japanese equivalents of European mushrooms such as hiratake (oyster mushroom family), maitake (hen of the wood), amigasatake (morel), amitake (boletus) and anzutake (chanterelle), as well as numerous regional seasonal varieties which are available locally.

BELOW: *Fresh shiitake mushrooms have a dark brown velvety cap and are ideal for grilling, frying or added to hotpots.*

FRESH SHIITAKE

Meaning tree (*shii*) mushroom, the shiitake is also known, incorrectly, as the Chinese mushroom, though it originated in Japan. Shiitake is a fungus that grows in the wild twice a year, in spring and autumn, under trees such as *shii* (*Pasania cuspidata*), oak and chestnut, though today it is also cultivated. It is recognized as a health food for its ability to reduce cholesterol in the blood.

Aroma and flavour

Fresh shiitake have a distinctive woody aroma and slightly acidic flavour. The mushroom has a soft, slippery texture, which adds an exquisite quality. When dried the flavour intensifies.

Culinary uses

The shiitake is one of the regular ingredients for hotpot dishes containing meat, usually beef, and vegetables, such as *shabu shabu* or *sukiyaki*. They can also be simply grilled over a barbecue or battered and fried for tempura.

Preparation and cooking

With a damp piece of kitchen paper wipe, rather than wash, off any earth and dirt, and trim off the hard part of the stem before cooking. When used whole, a decorative cross is often notched into the caps. Fresh shiitake can easily become too soft, so monitor the cooking carefully. Store fresh shiitake with the cap edges curled under, in the vegetable section of the refrigerator.

Grilled fresh shiitake with mustard

1 Wipe off the dirt from fresh shiitake with damp kitchen paper and use a small knife to trim off the hard parts of the stems.

2 Grill (broil) the mushrooms very lightly under a medium heat, or on a barbecue, for 1–2 minutes on both sides. Alternatively, heat a frying pan, add a little oil to just cover the base, and pan-fry the shiitake over a medium heat. Serve with mustard and shoyu.

Preparing dried shiitake

1 Quickly wash off any dirt from the mushrooms under running water and then soak in cold water. Dried shiitake must be soaked in tepid water for about 2–3 hours, or overnight, if you prefer. If you are short of time, you can soak for at least 45 minutes, with a little white sugar sprinkled over, before cooking.

2 Remove the shiitake from the soaking water, and gently squeeze out the water. Using your fingers or a knife, trim off the stem and then slice or chop the caps to use in cooking. Use the stems in soups. Don't discard the soaking liquid; rather drain through muslin (cheesecloth), then use in soups or for simmering.

DRIED SHIITAKE

When shiitake are dried, their aroma and flavour intensify; it is for this enriched fungus flavour, coupled with the convenience of using dried shiitake, that they are appreciated. There are many types and grades of dried shiitake available in packets, but the small, thick donko (winter mushroom) is the most highly rated. Dried shiitake last almost indefinitely if stored in an airtight plastic bag. They can also be frozen, which is a better way of retaining their flavour.

Aroma and flavour

Dried shiitake have a pleasantly strong, roasted aroma and intensified fungus flavour. The increased fibre content gives it more bite than fresh ones.

Culinary uses

In Japanese cooking, dried shiitake are usually cooked in a seasoned liquid, then used for dishes such as simmered vegetables with chicken, mixed sushi and soup noodles.

BELOW: *Various dried shiitake; on the far right are dried donko, which are considered the most flavoursome.*

ENOKITAKE

Also known as yukinoshita, meaning under the snow, this bundle of tiny berry-cap mushrooms with thin stems grows in the wild on the stumps of *enoki* (hackberry), poplar and persimmon trees in winter. Cultivated enokitake is often marketed outside Japan as a new nutritious salad ingredient to be eaten raw.

Aroma and flavour

Enokitake has a delicate, fresh flavour and a delightfully crisp texture.

Culinary uses

Enokitake are one of the regular ingredients for hotpot dishes, such as *shabu shabu*, and are also delicious in seasonal salads and in soups. They can also be eaten raw in salads.

Preparation and cooking

Cut off the spongy root of the mushroom, 2.5–5cm/1–2in from the bottom, and wash carefully. Use cooked or raw. They cook quickly, so do not overcook. Enokitake are the easiest mushroom to handle, and they give a refreshing character to dishes.

BELOW: *Cultivated enokitake.*

SHIMEJI

The shimeji is another popular Japanese mushroom and grows in autumn in bunches or in circles under trees such as *nara* (Japanese oak) and red pine. There are many varieties, but the most common has a light grey cap and grows to 2.5–10cm/1–4in in diameter. It is this variety that is most commonly available in the West from Asian supermarkets.

Shimeji keep for up to a week if stored in the vegetable compartment of the refrigerator. They can be stored dried, frozen and pickled.

Aroma and flavour

The shimeji has little aroma and an undistinguished flavour. Rather than for its taste, the shimeji is valued for its fresh, meaty texture which is thought to be similar to that of oyster mushrooms.

Culinary uses

This mushroom's fresh and unassuming character suits most delicate Japanese cooking, such as *shimeji gohan* (rice cooked with shimeji), clear soup, and grilled (broiled) and fried dishes. It is also a popular hotpot ingredient.

Preparation and cooking

Trim off the spongy part about 2–2.5cm/³⁄₄–1in from the bottom and quickly rinse the shimeji under cold running water. Using your fingers, separate the stem and cook lightly.

ABOVE: *Shaka shimeji are a popular variety of shimeji due to their striking and distinctive appearance.*

BELOW: *Oyster mushrooms have a similar texture to shimeji, and can be substituted if the latter are not available.*

Preparing shimeji

Wash or brush the mushrooms lightly with kitchen paper or a brush to remove any dirt particles. Cut off the hard base and separate any large blocks of fresh shimeji into smaller chunks with your fingers.

Seaweeds

The Japanese have been enjoying the bounty of their surrounding seas since ancient times, whether for fish, shellfish or seaweeds. Over 30 varieties of seaweeds plus the numerous products developed from them are regularly used in Japanese cooking. Most seaweeds contain iron, calcium, phosphorus and iodine and are rich in vitamins A and C.

KONBU

This giant kelp is an indispensable ingredient in Japanese cooking. It is used on its own and also provides a subtle flavour to numerous dishes as one of the basic ingredients of dashi (fish stock). It is rich in iodine, calcium and vegetable fibre.

Konbu grows in the northern seas off the Japanese coast, and Hokkaido, the northernmost island, is known as the biggest producer of dried konbu. There are many varieties of kelp; the size alone ranges from 5cm/2in to 30cm/12in wide and some grow to over 20m/60ft long. They are all dried and graded, classified by their uses, either for eating or for making dashi stock.

Dried konbu is also commercially processed to make numerous konbu by-products, such as cut konbu for savoury snacks and *tsukudani* (a slow-simmered savoury dish).

Aroma and flavour

Dried konbu has a distinctive ocean aroma and intense flavour. It has a pleasantly moist texture.

Culinary uses

The most important role dried konbu plays in Japanese cooking is in making dashi stock, together with katsuo-bushi (dried skipjack tuna flakes).

Preparation and cooking

Dried konbu is usually covered with a fine white powder, a natural by-product of the drying process. Do not wash or rinse off; instead, wipe with a piece of damp kitchen paper. In cooking, such as in soup or a hotpot, dried konbu sheet is made into decorative knots or rolled. Use the konbu's soaking water in either a stock or in a soup.

LEFT: *Oboro konbu is a thin sheet that is used for wrapping rice.*

Knotting and rolling konbu

1 To knot konbu, soak a sheet of konbu in a bowl of tepid water until it is soft. Cut the softened konbu crossways into 16cm/6¼in sheets, then cut lengthways into 2–3cm/¾–1¼in wide strips. Carefully make a knot in the centre of each konbu strip and cook.

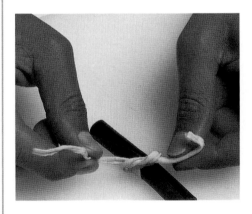

2 To roll knobu, cut a soaked konbu sheet crossways into 5cm/2in sheets and roll up tightly. A strip of carrot, an anchovy fillet, or thin strips of meat such as ham or sausage, can be rolled inside, if you wish. To secure the roll and prevent it from unravelling, tie neatly with a very thin strip of oboro konbu that has been soaked until soft.

NORI

The most famous seaweed product is nori, a dried paper-thin sheet of asakusa-nori, a laver, which is a small orange-brown, film-like marine algae. It grows up to 25cm/10in long and about 5cm/2in wide. The laver is washed in fresh water, laid in thin sheets and then sun-dried on bamboo or wooden frames.

Nori is rich in vegetable protein, vitamins and minerals. It is a packaged in a standard size of about 20 x 18cm/8 x 7in for rolling sushi, usually in packets of five or ten sheets. Mini nori sheets, about 8 x 3cm/3$^1/_2$ x 1$^1/_4$in are also available. These are used for wrapping rice, most notably served at a traditional breakfast, and some are ready-toasted or coated with a shoyu-based seasoning. Standard nori sheets are widely available from most large supermarkets and other types of nori can be found at Asian supermarkets.

Nori will keep almost indefinitely in an airtight bag placed in a container. Under no circumstances allow it to become moist.

Aroma and flavour

Although it has a light, smoky flavour, nori is mainly appreciated for its subtle ocean aroma. Dark, shiny nori has much more flavour than the cheaper reddish types.

Culinary uses

Nori is mainly used with rice for rolling sushi and wrapping *onigiri* (rice balls) and mochi (rice cakes). It can also be crumbled or shredded for use as a garnish on sushi or noodles.

Preparation and cooking

To bring out the aroma and make nori crispy, toast it on both sides before use by holding a sheet horizontally over a low heat. Move it about as you toast it so that it heats evenly. Watch it carefully as it will be very crisp within only 2–3 seconds. Do not grill (broil). One side of the nori sheet is shinier than the other, so when you make sushi, place the nori sheet shiny-side down on the makisu (sushi rolling mat) so the dull side is inside.

BELOW: *Nori sheets are ideal for making hand-rolled sushi.*

WAKAME

This is a brownish orange algae and grows up to 1–2m/3–6ft long on rocks under the sea from early winter through to early summer. Wakame is mostly dried or salted, and there are various types, sizes and grades of wakame readily available. Fresh wakame is available only in Japan, but processed wakame has been developed in recent years.

You can store dried wakame almost indefinitely in an airtight bag in a cool place away from direct sunlight.

Aroma and flavour

This seaweed has a delicate aroma and a very refreshing flavour. It is slightly slippery but has a pleasant vegetable crispness.

Culinary uses

Wakame is one of the most popular soup ingredients and is also delicious served as a salad with a vinegary dressing. It is often simmered with other vegetables.

Preparation and cooking

Dried wakame must be softened before use. If using a whole wakame with the stem intact, soak in tepid water for 15–20 minutes before cutting it out.

If using instant wakame, soak in plenty of water for about 5 minutes before use. Drain and pour boiling water over it, then immediately plunge into cold water. Some types of dried wakame can be put directly into the soup.

HIJIKI

Very popular among health-conscious eaters, hijiki is a twiggy black marine algae that grows up to 1m/3ft long all around the Japanese coast. It is full of vitamins, minerals, including calcium, and fibre, and contains no fat. Hijiki is cooked and dried, and sold in packets. It can be bought from Asian and Japanese grocery stores.

Aroma and flavour

Hijiki has little aroma and a faint ocean flavour. It also has a fairly tough texture.

Culinary uses

Hijiki is normally shallow-fried and then simmered in a shoyu-based sauce with other vegetables. It is often used with abura-age (fried thin tofu). It is also used to garnish rice dishes, such as mixed sushi and *onigiri* (rice balls), as its black, small twig-like shape provides an attractive contrast to the white rice.

Preparation and cooking

Soak dried hijiki in tepid water for 15–20 minutes until softened. It will normally expand to 7–10 times its dried volume. It goes well with oil, so it is often shallow-fried and then simmered in dashi-based soup seasoned with shoyu, mirin and sugar.

BELOW: *Hijiki seaweed can withstand vigorous cooking and it will keep well in an airtight container.*

ABOVE: *Dried and cut wakame, in a bowl. It is advisable to store dried wakame in an airtight bag in a cool place, away from direct sunlight.*

Herbs and spices

Unlike European cooking, where herbs and spices are cooked together with the main ingredients, Japanese cooking uses them mainly for additional aroma and flavour, often sprinkled on top of dishes or mixed with a dipping sauce.

Shiso, ginger and wasabi are some well-known examples, but there are also various wild plants called sansai, meaning literally mountain vegetables, which are used as herbs and spices for their unique aromas and flavours. These are, unfortunately, difficult to find outside of Japan.

SHISO

Although originally from China, Burma and the Himalayas, shiso has been cultivated in Japan for centuries, and is now used predominantly in Japanese cooking. Shiso is a member of the mint family and is also known as perilla. There are two types, green and red, and the whole shiso plant from berries to flowers is used as a herb or garnish for Japanese dishes. It is widely cultivated in the West. Green leaves in packets are sold all year round at Asian stores.

Aroma and flavour

The essential oils in shiso provide a very distinctive, pungent aroma and rich but subtly piercing flavour, which is more like basil than mint.

ABOVE: *Shiso has a pungent aroma and is perfect used as a garnish for tempura.*

Culinary uses

Normally only green shiso, with its exquisite flavour, is used as a herb and garnish for dishes such as *sashimi*, tempura and vinegared salads. Red shiso (known as the beefsteak plant in the United States) is used for making umeboshi (dried and salted Japanese apricot) and other pickles. The berries, stems and flowers of both types are also used to garnish *sashimi*, soup and sauces.

Preparation and cooking

Shiso is simply used as it is or cut into required shapes. If used for tempura, only the underside of the leaves should be battered and fried very quickly until they are crisp.

RIGHT: *Mitsuba looks similar to coriander (cilantro). The leaves are mainly used to impart a delicate flavour to clear soup or hors d'oeuvres.*

MITSUBA

This herb has three light green, coriander-like leaves (hence the name, meaning three leaves) on top of thin whitish stalks, about 15–20cm/6–8in long. A member of the parsley family, it is cultivated outside Japan and is available from Asian stores.

Aroma and flavour

Mitsuba has a relatively strong grass aroma and a faintly bitter flavour.

Culinary uses

Mitsuba is used for its unique aroma, so only a few leaves are put into clear soup, thick egg soup or used in hors d'oeuvres. It is also used for hotpot dishes and the stalks can be fried. Use the stalks to tie food – plunge into boiling water to make flexible.

Preparation and cooking

This is a very delicate herb so requires only very light par-boiling.

LEFT: *Pickled thinly sliced ginger, gari, is available in packets or jars, but can also be made at home.*

Culinary uses

Wasabi and raw fish are an inseparable combination and wasabi paste is always used for *sashimi* and sushi. Wasabi is also used for pickling vegetables and in salad dressings.

SHOGA

Fresh ginger, or shoga, is one of the oldest, most universal ingredients and dried root ginger is widely available all the year round. For Japanese cooking, however, only fresh ginger is used and often only the extracted juice. In addition to shoga (root ginger), so-called ha-shoga (ginger shoot), and mé-shoga (ginger sprout), are available in summer in Japan.

Aroma and flavour

Fresh ginger has a subtly pungent aroma, reminiscent of citrus, and a pleasantly sharp flavour. Young ginger is tender and mild enough to be cooked as a vegetable while older roots become fibrous and more pungent.

Culinary uses

Apart from pickled ginger to accompany sushi, root ginger is almost always grated and only the juice is used in Japanese cooking. Ginger shoot is also pickled and used as a garnish for grilled (broiled) fish dishes. Ginger sprout is mild enough to eat raw with miso, or to use for tempura.

Preparation and cooking

Always peel off the outer skin. To extract the juice, use a Japanese grater or fine cheese grater to finely grate the ginger, then squeeze out the juice. To make pickled ginger, use very fresh young root ginger, or ginger shoot.

WASABI

For over a thousand years, Japan's somewhat moderately flavoured cooking has been given an unusual pungency through the addition of wasabi. Meaning mountain hollyhock, it is sometimes introduced as the Japanese equivalent of Western horseradish, but they aren't related.

Grated fresh wasabi has a milder fragrance and less sharp pungency than horseradish. It is a rarity even in Japan and the root is more commonly used in its powdered and paste forms.

Aroma and flavour

Freshly grated wasabi has a refreshing, radish-like aroma and subtly pungent flavour. Interestingly, to give it a little more kick, white horseradish is also included, among other ingredients, to make the powders and pastes.

Making wasabi paste

Put about 5ml/1 tsp powdered wasabi in an egg cup and add the same volume of tepid water. Stir vigorously to make a firm, clay-like paste. Place the dish upside down on a board and leave to stand for at least 10 minutes before use. This will prevent the wasabi paste from drying out and at the same time helps it develop its distinctive sharp flavour.

ABOVE: *The root of the wasabi is made into a powder or paste and gives a pungent flavour to many Japanese dishes.*

Fish

There is no doubt that the Japanese are the world's biggest fish eaters. They deal with 3,000 kinds of fish and shellfish daily at the Tokyo fish market. Choices are far greater in Japan than anywhere else in the world and housewives go shopping for fresh fish every day.

MAGURO

A member of the mackerel family, maguro or tuna has become widely available in the West. There are several kinds of tuna: blue-fin (black tuna in Japan), big-eye, yellow-fin, long-finned and southern blue-fin. Katsuo, skipjack tuna is in the same family, but in a different group of fish.

Tuna is often sold already skinned and sliced as steaks or in chunks, which can make it sometimes difficult to tell which tuna you are buying.

In Japan, tuna is normally displayed cut into thick rectangular pieces –

BELOW: *Maguro intended for* sashimi *is classified according to which part of the fish it is from and its oiliness.*

convenient for *sashimi*. There are usually two kinds, akami and toro, depending on which part of the fish the flesh comes from. Akami, red meat, is from the main, upper part of the body and toro, oily meat, is from the lower.

Maguro is most often used for *sashimi* and sushi, salads, grilling (broiling), and *teriyaki*. Long-finned tuna is not consumed raw, but is sold canned as steaks.

ABOVE: *Fresh sake (salmon), a popular ingredient for* sashimi *in the West, and ikura (salmon caviar).*

SLICING FISH FOR *SASHIMI* AND SUSHI

Fish that can be eaten raw include tuna, skipjack tuna, salmon, mackerel, turbot, sea bass and sea bream. Use absolutely fresh fish and avoid ready-cut steaks or filleted fish. Also, do not eat defrosted frozen fish raw.

Slicing smaller or flat fish

Using a very sharp knife, fillet and skin the fish carefully, then carefully remove all the bones, including the fine bones from the fillets. If necessary use a pair of tweezers.

Using a sharp knife, cut flat fish fillets in half down the centre, then carefully slice very thinly, making sure that the blade of the knife is inserted diagonally. Do be careful not to cut your fingers.

Slicing tuna, skipjack tuna or salmon

Make sure you buy a chunky piece of fish, avoiding the part with the veins. Cut the chunk into 2–3cm/³⁄₄–1¹⁄₄in thick, 6–7cm/2¹⁄₂–2³⁄₄in wide fillets.

To cut into slices suitable for sushi, cut 5mm/¹⁄₄in thin slices crossways, placing the knife's blade slightly at an angle against the chopping board. For sashimi, slice 1cm/¹⁄₂in thick pieces, again keeping the blade slightly at an angle.

SAKE

While sake refers to salmon only, salmon and trout are categorized in the same group of fish although, rather confusingly, some salmon such as chinook (*Onorhynchus tshawytscha*), cherry (*O. masou masou*) and pink (*O. gorbuscha*) are regarded as trout in Japan. The king of salmon in Japan is chum salmon (*O. keta*), which has a perfect silvery body. It comes back to the river of its birth for spawning from September to January.

Salmon is used for *sashimi* in the West but, due to parasite infestation, not in Japan. For *sashimi*, ask the fishmonger to cut fresh from a big chunk of salmon rather than use ready-cut steaks.

In Japan, salmon is traditionally often salted and wrapped in an aramaki (straw mat). Fresh salmon is used for grilling (broiling), frying, *saka-mushi* (sake steaming), hotpots and soup dishes.

LEFT: *Whole and filleted suzuki (sea bass) is appreciated for its delicate flavour and chunky texture.*

Filleting and skinning round fish

1 Scale and gut the fish, cut off the head and wash under running water. Pat dry with kitchen paper and place the fish flat on a chopping board.

2 Insert a sharp knife as close as possible to the backbone. Cut along the back towards the tail keeping the knife flat to the bone.

3 Turn the fish over and repeat to fillet the other side. Place one fillet at a time skin-side down on the chopping board and insert the blade between the skin and meat at the tail end.

4 Press the skin firmly down with one hand and slowly push the blade, at an angle to the fish, along the skin towards the head to remove the skin. Discard the skin.

SUZUKI

The sea bass grows to about 1m/3ft long and tastes better when over 60cm/24in. It lives around the coast and estuaries of Japan. Suzuki is a handsome fish with big round eyes, a blue-grey back and silvery white belly. The pinkish white flesh, together with the delicate flavour and the chunky texture, adds a pleasant freshness to *sashimi* and sushi. If suzuki is to be cooked, it should be done so very lightly with sauce, in soup, steamed, grilled (broiled) or in a hotpot and make sure it is not overcooked. The flesh is far too delicate to be fried.

Sea bass are available all year round, as whole fish or as fillets. They are at their best in spring and early summer, before they spawn. The tastiest specimens are wild, but farmed suzuki are acceptable if wild bass is not available.

TAI

In Japanese cooking, sea bream, or tai, has a special place as a celebratory fish simply because the ending of the Japanese word for "celebration" sounds the same. The largest tai grow to 1m/3ft long but it is the 30–50cm/12–20in fish that is used whole for grilling (broiling). The flesh of tai is milky white and flaky when it is cooked so it is used for making soboro (fish flakes). It is also used for *sashimi* and sushi – such as *oshi zushi* (pressed sushi) – as well as in soups and rice dishes.

KAREI

There are more than 100 species of the karei family worldwide, including plaice, sole, halibut and flounder, and 20 of these inhabit the seas around Japan. Karei look very similar to hirame (see below) except chiefly for the location of the eyes: karei have eyes on the right-hand side of the body and hirame on the left.

BELOW: *Red and black tai (sea bream). The flavour and texture of black tai is similar to red, but not as fine.*

Depending on the species the texture and flesh can vary greatly. Sole is arguably the finest fish of the group, with a firm, delicate flesh and superb flavour. Karei are a very versatile fish and are used for *sashimi*, as well as pan-frying, simmering and also grilling (broiling).

HIRAME

A type of flounder, hirame is a flat fish with its eyes on the back. It is one of the most commonly used fish in Japanese cooking, being used for *sashimi* and sushi as well as for frying, simmering and steaming, and in vinegared vegetable dishes and dressed salads. The thin, broad chain-like frill on the edges of the fish, called *engawa*, is regarded as a delicacy and is used for *sashimi*, simmered and grilled dishes. You can substitute turbot or lemon sole, if you wish.

AJI

This is the general term for about 50 species of a group of fish ranging from horse mackerel to scad, which are now often available at good fishmongers in the West.

Very fresh aji is made into *tataki*, finely chopped flesh eaten with shoyu and grated fresh root ginger. It is also used for grilling (broiling), simmering, and in vinegared dishes. Smaller fish is good for frying whole. Aji is also famous for its dried products such as *hiraki-boshi* (the whole body is opened and dried) and *mirin-boshi* (a whole opened body dried with mirin) and *kusaya* (a strong smelling, opened dried body). Dried aji are available from Asian supermarkets.

BELOW: *Karei is a family of fish that includes plaice, sole, halibut and flounder. Aji (bottom right) is in the mackerel family.*

ANKOH

Monkfish or anglerfish, known as ankoh in Japan, is highly symbolic of winter in Japanese culinary terms. Fugu and puffer are similar winter fish.

A popular fish, ankoh is cooked in a hotpot at the table in restaurants as well as at home. It has a firm, chunky meat, not flaky even when cooked, so it is suitable for simmering, pan-frying or grilling.

In Japan all the parts of the ankoh, including the liver, stomach and ovaries, are eaten but the liver is regarded as a particular delicacy and is often compared to foie gras. The liver is normally marinated in a vinegar sauce and served as *sashimi*. Like many fish, ankoh is an excellent low-fat, low cholesterol source of protein and B vitamins.

BELOW: *The firm, chunky flesh of ankoh makes this fish ideal for most forms of cooking.*

IWASHI

Sardines, iwashi, are the most commonly used fish in Japan, and they account for 25 per cent of the total catch by the sea fisheries. Iwashi is best in winter but is available all year round.

Fresh iwashi is eaten grilled (broiled), in vinegared dishes, in mixed sushi, fried and minced (ground) into fish balls. However, it is mostly processed to make canned and numerous dried products such as niboshi, which is used for making dashi stock, and mezashi, four to six small half-dried iwashi strung together in a row with a small piece of straw.

In the past, export of these fish has been limited, but some are now produced in the West and are available from Japanese supermarkets.

SAMMA

Also known as saury, this long, narrow fish has a blue-black back and shiny silver-white belly. It inhabits the seas around North America and Russia, coming down towards Japan in autumn, the best time to eat it since by then it has acquired its maximum fat content of 20 per cent.

In autumn, samma is best grilled (broiled) or pan-fried whole and eaten with a little grated daikon and shoyu to moderate its fishy smell. Dried samma is also very popular. In other seasons when it is less oily, fresh samma is used for making vinegared salads or sushi.

Fresh samma is sold in season at high-quality fishmongers, and cooked samma in cans is often available.

BELOW: *Beheaded and gutted iwashi (sardines) are packed raw, with their backbones, in oil; the canning process cooks them. Samma (bottom left) is used for sushi, for cooking and for canning.*

Shellfish

Along with fish, shellfish have always been an indispensable ingredient in Japanese cooking, and Japan probably consumes the widest range of shellfish in the world. Most types are used for sashimi *and* sushi *as well as in other forms of cooking.*

EBI

Among the numerous kinds of shellfish used in Japanese cooking, the prawn has the largest market share. If you want to eat prawn sushi, for instance, at a sushi restaurant in Japan, you need to specify which prawn you would like from among at least five kinds likely to be available. Kuruma-ebi (tiger prawn) has a light reddish shell with brown or blue-red stripes and grows to about 20cm/8in long. Ushi-ebi (black tiger prawn) has a dark grey shell with black stripes and, along with kuruma-ebi, supposedly has the best flavour. Both are best eaten raw when very fresh but are also used for grilling (broiling), simmering, frying and in soups.

Korai-egi (Chinese prawn), also known as taisho-ebi, has a light grey shell. This prawn is used for tempura and other frying dishes, stir-frying or simmering.

Japanese shrimp, such as shiba-ebi and botan-ebi, are used mainly for cooking, and hokkoku aka-ebi, also known as ama-ebi, is a delicious sushi topping. Tenaga-ebi (freshwater shrimp) has long tentacles and is often used for simmering and frying, while even smaller shrimps, sakura-ebi, are mostly dried. Unfortunately, many of these are not available outside of Japan.

Preparation and cooking

In Japan all prawns and shrimp are available fresh, sometimes still alive, but in the West, they generally come onto the market frozen. When cooking prawns, leave them in their shells so that they won't lose too much of their flavour. When cooked, they turn bright red or pink.

Note

In the US all prawns are called shrimp, then differentiated according to size: small, medium, jumbo. The Japanese, however, use both shrimp and prawn, so US equivalents in brackets are provided, to avoid confusion.

BELOW: *Ushi-ebi (black tiger prawns) are considered the most flavoursome type of prawn of all. Cooked shrimp turn pink (right).*

ISE-EBI

The Japanese spiny lobster, ise-ebi has a brown or reddish purple shell and smaller claws than most American and European lobsters. It grows off the Pacific coast of west Japan to about 35cm/14in, though it also inhabits the seas around the Caribbean, Australia and Africa. Ise-ebi is traditionally used for celebratory meals because the red colour, when cooked, signifies happiness in Japan.

Lobsters have a uniquely firm, sweet flesh with a delicious flavour. Fresh ones are nearly always eaten as *sashimi*. At fish restaurants they are often kept in a tank and the chef makes a dish called *iki-zukuri* (live *sashimi*) from your choice of lobster in front of you.

RIGHT: *Tabara-gani (king crab) claws are extremely good to eat, especially in salads and fried dishes.*

BELOW: *Fresh ise-ebi, the Japanese spiny lobster are almost always eaten as* sashimi *in restaurants.*

KANI

There are about 1,000 different crabs inhabiting the seas around Japan alone. The commonest are tabara-gani (king crab), kegani (horsehair crab) and zuwai-gani (snow crab). As its intestine goes off very quickly, kani is always boiled or steamed, often as soon as it is caught on board the fishing boat, before going to market. King crabs look like gigantic spiny spiders, but are very good to eat.

The claw flesh is the main part eaten, most often fresh with citrus shoyu, in salads, in grilled (broiled) and fried dishes, or in hotpots. Crab meat is also one of the major ingredients for sushi. However, in cooked dishes canned crab meat is more usually used.

JAPANESE DELICACIES

Kani-miso Crab intestine mixture, is considered a delicacy in Japan and is most often served as part of an hors d'oeuvres tray or as an accompaniment to sake. Kani-miso is available canned.

Snow crab The sweet-tasting flesh of this crab is usually sold frozen or canned. The snow crab itself has a roundish pinkish-brown body and long legs. It is also known as the queen of the crabs.

IKA

Several types of squid are used in Japanese cooking. Taste, texture, colour and availability decide which one is used for a dish. Fresh squid is used for *sashimi* only if it is very fresh. Always cook squid lightly because overcooked squid is tough and chewy. Whole squid is also used for making *ika-zushi* (ika stuffed with sushi rice).

SQUID PRODUCTS

There are various squid products in Japan, which can increasingly be found at specialist stores in the West.

Surume

This is whole squid opened up and dried, and is one of a number of delicacies served to accompany drinks. It is normally grilled (broiled)

whole, torn crossways with the fingers into fine shreds, and eaten sprinkled with a little shoyu. Kensaki-ika (swordtip squid), with its fine, tender flesh, is the best. It is available in packets, either whole or shredded, from Japanese supermarkets.

Shiokara

This is raw squid, marinated in its own ink and salt. It is served with drinks or rice and is available in jars.

Matsumae-zuke

Another delicacy from the Kansai region, matsumae-zuke is made of surume (dried squid), konbu (kelp seaweed) and carrot shreds marinated in a mixture of mirin and shoyu. It is also served with freshly cooked rice or as an appetizer with drinks. When

BELOW: *Surume (dried squid).*

time is short, make-your-own packets, which contain all the ingredients for matsumae-zuke pre-prepared, can be bought from Japanese supermarkets.

Preparing squid

1 Rinse the squid thoroughly under cold running water. Put your fingers carefully inside the body, grab all the tentacles, together with the soft central bone and intestine, and gently pull everything out of the cavity.

2 Separate the flaps from the body so the white flesh comes away. Peel off the skin. Cut away the intestine. Cut off the tentacles and rub off the skin.

3 For *sashimi*, cut the body flesh in half lengthways and then slice each piece crossways into thin strips to reduce its chewy texture.

4 For geso (tentacle *sashimi*), divide the ten tentacles into five equal pieces or separate individually, and cut the two long feelers in half.

5 For tempura, pan-frying and grilling (broiling), make criss-cross slits on the skin side of the body of the squid then cut into several pieces.

TAKO

There are over ten types of octopus caught all over the world and their sizes vary from Idako (baby octopuses), which are less than 10cm/4in, to ones over 3m/10ft. The most common octopus are in the *ma-dako* family.

Japanese cooking uses the octopus' eight tentacles, lightly blanched, for *sashimi* and vinegared salad dishes. Octopus is also used in hotpots, oden in particular, and for making an ink-marinated delicacy to accompany drinks. Prepared tentacles are available from fish counters in Japanese stores.

HAMAGURI

Clams are one of the oldest foods in Japan as is evident from the remains of the shells found in all the prehistoric settlements excavated. They are still a very important ingredient, and many varieties are used for Japanese cooking such as aka-gai (ark shell), asari (Manila clam), tori-gai (cockle), baka-gai or aoyagi (hen clam) and hokki-gai (surf clam). They are all used for sushi and *sashimi* as well as for all other methods of cooking.

HOTATE-GAI

The scallop is a very versatile shellfish because of its size and fish-like texture. There are several members of the scallop family available in Japan, including hotate-gai, the scallop most often sold in the West; itaya-gai (Japanese scallop), tsukihi-gai (saucer scallop) and hiogi-gai (noble scallop). All varieties are regular ingredients for sushi and *sashimi*. They are used for vinegared salads, or can be salt-grilled, simmered, fried or used in soups. The thin ribbon around the scallop's flesh and the red intestine are not wasted. Dried scallop is available from Asian supermarkets and some larger stores.

ABOVE: *Kaki, pacific oysters, are available in Japan all year round but they are most flavoursome from November to March.*

KAKI

A few Pacific oysters are available in Japan. The most common kaki (giant Pacific oyster) is oblong in shape, about 8cm/3½in long and 5cm/2in wide in contrast to the round European native oyster.

To eat oyster raw, Japanese-style, dip in a little citrus shoyu. *Kaki-fry* (fried breaded oyster) is another Japanese speciality. Oysters are also used in clear soups, hotpots and cooked with rice. Kaki are known to cause food poisoning so when eaten raw they should be as fresh as possible. Always buy fresh oysters from a reputable fishmonger.

BELOW: *Large hamaguri (common hard clams) and asari (Manila clams) are just two of the many clams that are used in Japanese cooking.*

BELOW: *Dried hotate-gai (scallops) are soaked in a little sake and steamed to make them soft and easy to handle. This process also brings out their distinctive flavour.*

BELOW: *Fresh cockles (tori-gai) are often used for sushi.*

Fish roes

The Japanese use all parts of the fish, and its eggs, in particular, are regarded as a delicacy. Since the eggs are normally heavily salted to preserve them, they go well with plain boiled rice. They are also regular ingredients in sushi and are used for making hors d'oeuvres.

TARAKO

Cod ovaries, called tarako, are available at the fish counters of supermarkets in Japan. Sold in pairs, cod ovaries are usually simply grilled (broiled) to eat with boiled rice.

IKURA

In Russia, all fish eggs are called ikura, but the name is used only for salmon eggs in Japan. Ikura is already salted to preserve it, so it normally keeps for a short time. It is mainly used for sushi, eaten with grated daikon and

hoyu, and also for making hors d'oeuvres. It is widely available in jars at supermarkets.

KAZUNOKO

Salted and dried herring ovaries, kazunoko, were once abundant but are now so scarce that they have become a rare delicacy. Soak in water overnight to soften and remove the salt before use. Kazunoko is usually eaten as it is with a little shoyu and katsuo-bushi, dried skipjack tuna flakes.

UNI

The Japanese sea urchin, or uni, is a dark spiky, round sea creature that varies in size, depending on type, from 3–4cm/1¼–1½in to over 10cm/4in in diameter. Only the ovaries of the uni are eaten. Fresh uni is one of the regular items for sushi toppings and is also used for making hors d'oeuvres. Salted uni is also available.

ABOVE: *Kazunoko (salted and dried herring ovaries).*

Look for urchins with firm spines and a tightly closed mouth (on the underside). To open, wear gloves and use a purpose-made knife, though sharp scissors can also be used. Cut into the soft tissue around the mouth and lift off the top to reveal the coral.

Alternatively, slice off the top like a boiled egg. Remove the mouth and innards, which are inedible, but retain the rich juices for use in sauces. Scoop out the bright orange coral.

LEFT: *Ikura (salmon caviar).*

BELOW: *Uni (Japanese sea urchin ovaries).*

BELOW: *Tarako (cod ovaries) are usually slightly red, front. Tarako with chilli is brighter red (back).*

Fish products

Numerous fish products are used in Japanese cooking and many are available in the West, fresh or frozen. They are easy to use and very useful as a flavouring in home-cooking.

BELOW: *Unagi no kabayaki, grilled eel, is served with rice and seven-spice chilli powder.*

KATSUO-BUSHI

Katsuo, skipjack tuna, is cooked and dried whole to a hard block called katsuo-bushi and then shaved for use. Ready-shaved kezuri-bushi or hanagatsuo in various graded packets is widely available. This is one of the main ingredients in dashi stock and is also used for sprinkling on vegetables or fish as an additional flavouring. Mixed with a little shoyu, it makes a delicious accompaniment to hot boiled rice.

NIBOSHI

These hard, dried sardines are used for making a strong-flavoured dashi stock. In contrast to the delicate flavour of kezuri-bushi, niboshi is boiled for about 5 minutes to exude the flavour and make a more robust stock. Hence niboshi stock is used for making soups such as miso soup and the soup for soba and udon noodles.

UNAGI NO KABAYAKI

Filleted eel is steamed, then grilled (broiled) with a thick, sweet shoyu sauce. This soft fish does not resemble, or taste like, eel. It is placed on top of hot boiled rice with the accompanying sauce sprinkled with seven-spice chilli powder, or sansho. Most people buy unagi no kabayaki instead of making it themselves. It is available ready-to-eat in packets, frozen or vacuum-packed.

HIDARA

This dried cod fillet can be grilled, then torn into pieces with the fingers and eaten with rice. It is also used for making snacks to go with drinks, and is available in packets.

MEZASHI

Meaning eye-pierced, mezashi is made from half-dried whole sardines strung together, four to six at a time, by a piece of straw pierced through the eyes, hence the name. It is just lightly grilled and eaten with hot boiled rice or to accompany sake. Mezashi is sometimes available at larger Asian food stores.

SHISHAMO

This small, 10–15cm/4–6in long, narrow, pinkish silver fish is unique to the north Pacific and Atlantic oceans. Shishamo is considered one of the best Japanese delicacies to eat with sake, especially *komochi-shishamo* (shishamo with eggs), and this is priced accordingly.

CHIRIMEN-JAKO

A speciality of the Kansai region (Osaka and surrounds), these are another form of dried shirasu (white fry sardines), which have been cooked and often flavoured with shoyu. They are eaten as are and make a good accompaniment for hot rice or in *ochazuke* (cooked rice in tea). Shoyu-flavoured ones are fairly salty. They are available in packets in most Asian supermarkets.

TAZUKURI

Dried small sardines, tazukuri are lightly roasted in a small pan before serving as an accompaniment for drinks or as a snack. They have a distinctive *umami* (rich flavouring). At New Year's time they are coated in sugar and served as part of the savoury celebration hamper. Tazukuri are another fish product available outside of Japan.

Fish pastes

Numerous puréed fish products are used in Japanese cooking, among which the following are the most common. They are normally available frozen from Japanese food stores and are the main ingredients for oden *(fish pastes and vegetables cooked in dashi-based soup).*

KAMABOKO

Puréed white fish is mixed with a binding agent and made into various shapes and sizes then steamed, boiled or grilled (broiled) to produce kamaboko. The standard product is called ita-kamaboko, a small fish paste cake, about 4–5cm/$1^1/_2$–2in thick and 15cm/6in long, stuck on a wooden board. Eat kamaboko finely sliced with shoyu and mustard as an hors d'oeuvre.

SATSUMA-AGE

This is deep-fried kamaboko and is normally shaped into an oval disc measuring about 7.5 x 5cm/3 x 2in. Pour boiling water over the paste to reduce the oil before use. It can be eaten as it is with shoyu, or lightly grilled.

CHIKUWA

Puréed fish is moulded around a stick, then steamed and grilled, and the stick removed. Chikuwas normally measure about 15cm/6in long with the hole running this length. The outer skin is seared an attractive uneven brown. It can be eaten either just sliced, used for simmering with vegetables or added to hotpots.

NARUTOMAKI

This is a kind of kamaboko with a decorative pink swirling pattern inside, which is made by kneading dyed red fish meat into white meat.

Narutomaki is one of the regular ingredients for ramen, which are Chinese-style noodles, and it is also used in udon noodles and soups.

HANPEN

This puréed shark's flesh is mixed with grated yam and egg whites, shaped into a 7–8cm/$3^1/_2$–$3^3/_4$in square cake about 1cm/$1/_2$in thick and then boiled. It has a light, fluffy texture and can be eaten grilled with shoyu and mustard, and is also used for hotpots and soups.

TSUMIRE

This small, greyish coloured hand-rolled fish ball is made from red meat fish such as sardines and mackerel and, though firm, has a soft texture. It is a flat disc with a "crater" in the centre so that it heats quickly and evenly. Tsumire is used in soup, *oden* and hotpot dishes and is available frozen in specialist stores.

RIGHT: *Ita-kamaboko, white fish paste on a wooden board.*

LEFT: *Clockwise from left to right; satsuma-age, narutomaki, chikuwa, and hanpen puréed fish products.*

Meat and chicken

The eating of meat was banned in Japan for many years, first due to Buddhism and later by the Shogunate for 300 years until 1868. It was only after World War II that meat, mainly beef, pork and chicken became a part of the general diet. It is still used sparingly; usually thinly sliced or shredded and cooked with vegetables, or minced (ground).

BEEF
There are four types of *wagyu* (Japanese beef): black, reddish brown, hornless and short-horned. Black beef is the most common. Matsuzaka beef, also known as Kobe beef, omi beef and yonezawa beef, are the top-quality meats. They are given beer to drink, which helps to distribute the fat. *Wagyu* is not available in the West

but you can use sirloin or fillet instead. For *sukiyaki* and *shabu shabu*, where almost transparent slices are required, choose a roasting joint without a bone, or fillet. If a joint is used, trim off the fat completely and cut into 4–5cm/1½–2in thick oblong pieces, then freeze for two or three hours. Remove to the refrigerator, leave for 1 hour to half thaw and then slice into paper-thin oblong pieces. Ready-sliced *sukiyaki* beef is generally available from stores. Trim off any excess fat, if necessary.

PORK
Since ancient times pork has been eaten, even during the period when meat was banned, and it remains popular today. It is thinly sliced, pan-fried and mixed with grated fresh root

ginger and shoyu, or else chopped and used as a flavouring in vegetable dishes. Long-simmered pork is delicious with ramen.

CHICKEN
Native regional chickens, called jidori, are popular in Japan, though there are also many mass-produced broiler chickens. *Nagoya kochin* is one such jidori, with a pinkish golden, firm meat. Minced chicken is often used for making meatballs, sauces or as a flavouring for simmered vegetables. *Yakitori* is chicken pieces threaded on a bamboo skewer, then grilled (broiled) with sweet taré sauce. Boneless chicken thighs marinated in *teriyaki* sauce and then grilled are ideal for barbecues. Chicken is also used for hotpots.

LEFT: *Chicken is used in various ways; minced for making meatballs, skewered for* teriyaki, *and the thigh for barbecuing.*

ABOVE: *Finely sliced beef for* shabu shabu *and* sukiyaki.

RIGHT: *Thinly sliced pork is often pan-fried with fresh root ginger.*

Sauces

Shoyu and miso are the two oldest and most important flavouring sauces in Japanese cooking. Their strong, distinctive flavours mean that shoyu and miso are used more as condiments for dipping or as flavourings for cooking, rather than as sauces for coating food.

LEFT: *Light and dark shoyu. Use light shoyu, left, for flavouring, such as in clear soups, and dark shoyu, above back, in simmered dishes.*

Shoyu and miso have a preservative quality and are good for marinating raw fish, meat and vegetables. The Japanese have also developed ready-mixed sauces for dishes like *sukiyaki* and *yakiniku* (barbecue), as well as Japanese vinegar and mirin, both made from rice.

ABOVE: *Light shoyu (soy sauce), right, has a lighter colour but saltier flavour than regular shoyu, left.*

SHOYU

Japan's ancient seasoning was called hishio, and consisted of a preserve of what was at that time very scarce and precious salt fermented with animal or vegetable protein and fibre. Grain hishio, fermented with grains such as rice and wheat, and also beans, was developed into miso and its exuded liquid became shoyu. (The present-day sushi is also thought to derive from the ancient fish hishio, raw fish fermented with salt and rice.)

Using new techniques, introduced from China, Japan soon developed its own type of soy sauce, shoyu, made from daizu (soya beans), wheat and salt. Shoyu is now widely available from supermarkets, but Japanese shoyu is quite different in aroma and flavour from Chinese varieties.

Aroma and flavour

Shoyu is quite salty, although less salty now than it used to be, due to recent warnings about the role of salty food in heart disease. There are basically two types: usukuchi (light), and koikuchi (dark). The usukuchi is an all-purpose shoyu, clearer but slightly saltier than koikuchi, which is used for making sauces such as taré for *teriyaki*. There are also many grades, depending on the grade of soya beans, which are priced accordingly. Tamari is made from soya beans only without wheat, so it is similar to the liquid obtained during the making of miso.

Culinary uses

Shoyu is without doubt the single most important ingredient in Japanese cuisine and is used in almost every recipe. It is often used as a dip on its own for sushi, *sashimi*, pickles and many other dishes. Tamari is a dark shoyu used for making taré sauce and is suitable for those on a wheat-free diet.

MISO

Although lifestyles are rapidly changing, for many Japanese the day still starts with a bowl of miso soup for breakfast. Miso is one of the oldest traditional Japanese ingredients – it was already being made in the 12th century – and its origin can be traced back to the ancient seasoning called hishio, a preserve of salt fermented with grains and beans.

Numerous kinds and brands of miso are available in supermarkets, even outside Japan. They are categorized into three basic grades according to strength of flavour and colour: shiro-miso (white, light and made with rice), aka-miso (red, medium and made with barley), and kuro-miso (black, strong and made with soya beans).

Aroma and flavour

Miso is quite salty and has a strong fermented bean flavour. Shiro-miso is the lightest in saltiness and flavour, aka-miso is of medium flavour, and the strongest is kuro-miso. There are less salty brands available for the health conscious.

Culinary uses

Miso is a versatile ingredient and can be simply diluted with dashi stock to make soups, including the soup for miso ramen. It is used as seasoning for simmered dishes or dipping sauces, and also as a marinade for meat and fish. Shiro-miso (white) is a speciality of Kyoto, and it is good for soups, dressings and marinades. Aka-miso (red) is good for soups and for meat marinades. Hatcho-miso, the best kuro-miso (black), is rich and salty, and is good for dipping sauces and soups. It is often used mixed with another lighter miso. It loses its subtle aroma if overcooked.

BELOW: *Clockwise from top left, aka-miso, shiro-miso, hatcho-miso and kuro-miso.*

Miso-marinated flat fish or steak

Flat fish such as plaice and turbot are used for this dish, which involves marinating the fish in shiro-miso, a kind of white miso, which is made from rice and has a light flavour.

1 On a large plate spread a thin layer of shiro-miso (use aka-miso for meat). Cover with a piece of kitchen paper and press lightly so that the miso is absorbed by the paper.

2 Place the fish fillets, flesh side down, or meat on the kitchen paper and cover with another piece of kitchen paper.

3 Using a knife, press a thin layer of miso on top of the paper so that the paste covers the fish or meat. The paste will soak through and marinate the fish or meat. Leave the fish to marinate for about 3 hours or it can be marinated overnight, if you prefer.

4 Remove the fish or meat from the marinade and grill (broil) as required in the recipe.

Ready-made sauces

A number of ready-to-use ingredients have been developed in recent years and Japanese cooking is much easier as a result. The following ready-made sauces are available in the West.

MEN-TSUYU

This is a dashi-based condensed sauce for soba and udon noodles. It is made of dashi stock, shoyu, salt, sugar and other ingredients, and is used as a dipping sauce or soup for noodles. The instructions on the packet will state how much water should be added to make a dip for soba and somen, or soup in which to cook udon and soba. Men-tsuyu is most delicious when made a few hours in advance and left to sit so that the flavours can develop. It is usual to dilute 1:1 for a dip and 1:8 for soup. Store in the refrigerator.

TONKATSU SAUCE

Pork cutlet or tonkatsu is one of the most popular dishes in Japan, and this thick brown sauce is the ideal accompaniment, together with shredded cabbage and mustard. It is made of fruits, spices and seasonings. You can easily make your own tonkatsu sauce by mixing a fruit sauce, such as ketchup, and Worcestershire sauce.

TEN-TSUYU

This tasty dipping sauce for tempura is made of dashi stock, shoyu, mirin and a number of seasonings. Ten-tsuyu is normally used undiluted together with a little grated daikon and finely shredded fresh root ginger.

PONZU

Made of citrus juice, vinegar and seasonings, ponzu is used mixed with shoyu and spices for hotpot dishes. It is very tart in flavour with a watery consistency and yellow colour.

SUKIYAKI SAUCE

This is a sweet shoyu sauce for cooking *sukiyaki*, made of dashi stock, sugar, sake and seasonings. First thinly sliced beef is pan-fried, then some of this sauce is added, together with bitesize vegetables.

YAKINIKU NO TARÉ

This Japanese version of barbecue sauce is made of shoyu, spices and various seasonings. It is slightly sweeter than the Western barbecue sauces and is very good used for griddled food.

CURRY ROUX

Japan was first introduced to curry in the middle of the 19th century, not directly from India but via England,

LEFT: *Ponzu can be mixed with shoyu and used in hotpot dishes, such as beef.*

RIGHT:
Curry roux.

where curry powder was concocted and exported. Since then, curry has become one of the most popular daily foods in Japan. The Japanese, as with many introduced ingredients, further developed the powder into an instant curry sauce roux, mixing together all the necessary ingredients such as herbs and spices, fruits, soup stock, sauces and seasonings.

Curry roux comes in the form of a soft slab, resembling

a chocolate bar, in a sectioned plastic tray. All you need to do is boil the fresh ingredients such as meat or shellfish, potato, onion and carrot, and add some of this sauce mix. There are degrees of hotness: mild, medium, hot and very hot. There are also separate roux for meat and fish. An average packet normally serves 12, but remember that a Japanese portion is very small and it really makes enough for only six to eight adult appetites, particularly if eaten on its own.

Japanese curry is quite sweet, even the very hot type, and usually contains a lot of MSG (monosodium glutamate). If you are unsure of the flavour peculiar to MSG, which can make you a little thirsty afterwards, use this product very sparingly or omit altogether from the dish.

Making simple sauces at home

Most Japanese people have a number of sauces in their repertoire that can be easily and quickly made on the day of use.

Yuan sauce This sauce gives a subtle flavour to rather bland ingredients such as white fish, and also enhances the flavours of stronger-flavoured varieties, such as salmon. To make the sauce, mix together 5 parts mirin, 3 parts shoyu to 2 parts sake and 2 parts lime juice in a small bowl. Marinate the fish in the sauce for at least 15 minutes, before frying or cooking over a barbecue.

Tonkatsu sauce This is delicious with fried pork. To make the sauce, mix together 1 part Worcestershire sauce to 5 parts tomato ketchup in a small bowl. Coat some pork slices in a little flour then in some beaten egg and deep-fry briefly until cooked. Dip the fried pork into the sauce and eat immediately.

LEFT: *The numerous types of Japanese ready-made sauces include, from left, tonkatsu sauce, sukiyaki sauce, men-tsuyu sauce, ponzu, men-tsuyu sauce for somen and yakiniku no taré.*

Vinegars and **mirin**

Unlike shoyu and miso, Japanese vinegar and mirin (sweet cooking sake) are delicate tasting and good for adding subtle flavours to Japanese cooking. Both mirin and Japanese vinegar are made from rice.

RICE VINEGAR

Unless labelled yonezu (pure rice vinegar), most Japanese vinegars, called su or kokumotsu-su, normally contain other grains besides rice. Rice vinegar, other vinegars and vinegar products are all available at Japanese supermarkets.

Japanese rice vinegar has a mild, sweet aroma and is less sharp than ordinary wine vinegar.

Vinegar has many qualities. It can be used to refresh and soften saltiness, it acts as an antiseptic, and is a coagulant for proteins. It also prevents food from discolouring, helps to wash off slimy substances from food and to soften small fish bones. It is, therefore, useful from the preparation stage of food to the final seasoning. There are numerous vinegared dishes, such as cucumber and wakame salad, vinegar-cured raw fish, and gari (pickled ginger) to accompany sushi.

MIRIN

This amber-coloured, heavily sweetened sake is used only in cooking. It is one of Japan's ancient sake and is made from shochu (distilled sake). Shochu, mixed with steamed glutinous rice and koji (a yeast-like culture made from rice), is brewed and compressed to absorb the liquid, and then filtered.

Mirin has a faint sake aroma and syrupy texture, which adds not only a mild sweetness to food but also an attractive shiny glaze and slightly alcoholic flavour.

It is used for simmered dishes and in glazing sauces such as taré (for *yakitori*) and also for *teriyaki* sauce. Other uses include *mirin-boshi* (a mirin-coated dried fish), and daikon is pickled in mirin pulp.

Use mirin towards the end of the cooking time to add a subtle sweetness and depth to the flavour of the dish. It is not meant to be used as a sweetener, but if you must, you can use 5ml/1 tsp sugar in place of 15ml/1 tbsp mirin.

Both vinegar and mirin keep well for a long time if stored in a cool, dry place away from sunlight. It is best to use mirin within the stated time, since the flavour deteriorates.

ABOVE: *Yonezu (rice vinegar) and kokumotsu-su (grain vinegar).*

LEFT: *When buying rice vinegar, look for hon-mirin, left, rather than mirin-fuhmi, right, which is a cheap imitation.*

Dried flavourings

Ever on the look-out for delicious accompaniments to hot plain boiled rice, the Japanese have developed a number of dried flavourings. These are collectively known as tsukudani.

TSUKUDANI

Various foodstuffs, such as konbu (kelp seaweed), shiitake, matsutake, dried herring, clams, beef and even whale meat are made into tsukudani. Konbu is the most popular. It is cut into small pieces and then simmered with shoyu for a long time. It is sometimes cooked with other foods, such as shiitake or matsutake, and fish flakes. Tsukudani is fairly salty and goes well with hot plain boiled rice. Konbu tsukudani is usually available in packets from Japanese supermarkets all year round.

FURIKAKE

Consisting of various types of granulated fish and vegetable extracts, furikake are popular sprinkled on hot boiled rice. They are also used for making *onigiri* (rice balls), either mixed with rice or used as a stuffing. Various sprinkles come in packets or jars and are available from Japanese supermarkets.

ABOVE: *Assorted furikake (seafood and vegetable granules).*

OCHAZUKE NO MOTO

A favourite Japanese way of enhancing left-over rice is to pour over boiling water to which has been added a flavouring.

There are many different flavours of ochazuke no moto available, including salted salmon, cod roe, umeboshi (salted and dried Japanese apricots) and nori, and they are available from supermarkets in individual packets.

SUSHI MIX

This is a packet or jar of pre-prepared ingredients for *chirashi-zushi* (mixed sushi), which is made by stirring the packet's contents into cooked rice to make sushi rice. The garnish of shredded nori is also included in the packet. The flavour is sweet and it contains MSG (monosodium glutamate), which can leave you feeling very thirsty.

BELOW: *Ochazuke no moto (flavourings for left-over rice).*

BELOW: *Sushi mixes.*

Pickles

For the Japanese, rice and tsukemono (pickled vegetables) have gone hand in hand since ancient times. There are many varieties of tsukemono, also known as oshinko, preserved in all sorts of ways, and different regions have their own speciality.

Barrel after barrel of freshly made tsukemono are displayed in the food hall of any department store in Japan and you can sample them before buying. The Japanese do not use vinegar as a pickling agent; instead, rice bran, miso, sake or mirin pulps, mustard, koji (rice malt) or shoyu, together with salt, are used. Salting takes away the coarseness of the hard vegetables and makes them soft and digestible as well as preserving them. It also adds more character and depth to the taste and improves the nutritional content.

BELOW: *Shio-zuke (salt-pickled vegetables) can refer to a number of vegetables including, from left, aubergine, radish and cucumber.*

The following are some of the popular pickles available in packets from Japanese supermarkets and Asian grocery stores.

TAKUAN

Fresh, just harvested daikon are hung for two to three weeks, then salted and pickled in nuka (dry rice bran) and salt. It takes two or three months to mature and the end result is a soft but crunchy, delicious yellow daikon. This tsukemono is said to have been invented by the Buddhist monk Takuan in the 17th century, hence its name. Salty with a hint of sweetness, it is good on its own with hot boiled rice. It is also a regular ingredient for *nori-maki* (nori-rolled sushi) and other rice dishes. Most of the manufactured takuan has bright yellow food colouring added, so for naturally pickled daikon, look for the paler ones and check the label first.

SHIO-ZUKE

This is the general term used for all salted vegetables, and many vegetables, including cucumber, aubergine (eggplant), daikon, hakusai and mustard leaves, are used.

NARA-ZUKE

This tsukemono is a speciality of Nara, the ancient capital of Japan. The pulp that mirin is exuded from is used to pickle various vegetables, and nara-zuke (salted daikon pickled in mirin pulp) is one such pickle. It has a sweet flavour with a hint of alcohol.

NUKA-ZUKE

This is a traditional method of pickling and each household used to keep a tub of nuka-miso (rice bran mash), which resembles miso and from which it takes its name. Nuka (dry rice bran) is mixed with warm, strong brine into a mash, in which vegetables such as aubergine (eggplant), carrot, cucumber, daikon, hakusai or turnips are buried and left to pickle. It is ready to eat the next day.

This process makes the vegetables mildly sweet and enriches the flavour, but not without paying the price of its strong odour. The mash must be stirred every day, ideally with bare hands. Although long-serving dutiful wives were once fondly called nuka-miso (smelling wife), today not many wives wish to be appreciated for their smelly hands! Nuka for pickling is available from Japanese stores, although ready-pickled nuka-zuke in packets is more popular nowadays.

ABOVE: *Nara-zuke (mirin pulp pickles) is a speciality of Nara, the ancient capital of Japan and is eaten with boiled rice.*

MISO-ZUKE

The saltiness and strong flavour of miso are the two ideal qualities for making pickles, and the earliest known variety of Japanese pickle was made using miso. Red or white miso can be used on its own or often flavoured with mirin and sake to make miso-doko (miso mash). Fish and shellfish, poultry and beef can be marinated before grilling (broiling) and vegetables that have been marinated are then eaten as pickles.

All crunchy vegetables are suitable for pickling in miso but gobo (burdock root) is probably better than anything else for pickling in miso. Vegetables can be par-boiled beforehand to cut down on pickling time but the longer the vegetables rest in the miso, the more flavourful the pickle. Ready-to-eat gobo miso pickles are usually available in packets at Japanese supermarkets.

RAKKYO

To make rakkyo, spring onions (scallions) are first salted and then pickled in heavily sweetened vinegar. This is traditionally served with curry.

Making a pickled turnip flower

Serve these attractive flowers as an hors d'oeuvre or as a garnish for sushi.

1 Trim and peel five small turnips and place, one at a time, between a pair of hashi (chopsticks) on a cutting board.

Insert a very sharp blade down into the turnip, across the hashi, and make parallel cuts until the blade touches the hashi. Turn the turnip 90 degrees, and cut across the first series of cuts.

2 Repeat with the remaining turnips, then place them in a bowl. Sprinkle with 5ml/1 tsp salt and rub in lightly. Cover with a plate, place a weight on top and leave to stand for 30 minutes.

3 Mix 250ml/8fl oz/1 cup rice vinegar with 150g/5oz/¾ cup sugar in a bowl and stir until the sugar has dissolved. Drain the turnips and pour the vinegar mixture over them. Leave to marinate and soften overnight.

Making rice bran pickles

Nuka-zuke is a traditional pickling method for vegetables such as carrot, daikon and cucumber, and is an old Japanese favourite.

1 Following the instructions on the packet of nuka, mix the water and salt in a pan and bring to the boil. Remove the pan from the heat and leave to cool. The ratio is usually 3 parts nuka to 1 part of salt mixed with 2½ parts of water.

2 Put the rice bran in a large mixing bowl, then add the salted water and mix thoroughly. Seal well or transfer the wet nuka to a large container with a tight-fitting lid. Leave the nuka to settle for 5 days, stirring well about 1–2 times a day.

3 Wash and trim the vegetables (cut big vegetables into smaller sizes), then push them into the bran bed. Softer vegetables are ready within 24 hours and harder ones, such as daikon, within 2 days. Adjust the saltiness by adding more salt or rice bran. Stir the bran well every day even when nothing is being pickled. The bran can be used indefinitely.

Index